Uniquely Great

Uniquely Great

Essentials for Winning Employers

Lucy English, PhD

BEP BUSINESS EXPERT PRESS

Uniquely Great: Essentials for Winning Employers

First published in 2020 by
Business Expert Press, LLC
222 East 46th Street, New York, NY 10017
www.businessexpertpress.com

ISBN-13: 978-1-94897-606-0 (paperback)
ISBN-13: 978-1-94897-607-7 (e-book)

Business Expert Press Human Resource Management and
Organizational Behavior Collection

Collection ISSN: 1946-5637 (print)
Collection ISSN: 1946-5645 (electronic)

Cover design by Ana Marinovic, graphic designer
Interior design by Exeter Premedia Services Private Ltd., Chennai, India

First edition: 2020

10 9 8 7 6 5 4 3 2 1

Printed in the United States of America.

Abstract

Every organization is unique. In order to make yours the best it can be, you need to understand the concepts presented in this volume, and know what questions to ask as you explore the potential in front of you. There are oceans of information available about how to build a great organization. Trends in how to create culture, attract talent, and boost productivity seem to shift as quickly as seasons of the year. This volume provides a succinct overview of concepts related to organizational success, and offers a clear-eyed assessment of what is useful and what not. It guides you in questions to ask yourself, your leadership team, and employees of your organization so that you can make wise and informed decisions about how to proceed on the path to a uniquely great organization.

Keywords

Employer-of-choice; employee well-being; wellness; employee engagement; inclusion; corporate culture; work community; mental health; behavioral health; stress; burnout; resilience; leadership; work and family; continuous learning

Contents

Introduction

Creating great organizations is all about enabling people. I think of it as learning to use magic. Consider magic as the result of using our ordinary abilities to create extraordinary outcomes. It requires a great deal of intention, attention, and wisdom. Intention because we need to be clear about our motivations and desired outcomes, attention because it requires focus and effort, and wisdom because we have to choose carefully where we put those efforts. A well-chosen project to which we apply honest energy can result in magic. This book is about how to apply ordinary abilities to create extraordinary organizations. Doing this requires asking a lot of questions, because questions take you to new places, new understanding, and unforeseen possibilities.

In this volume I'll guide you to ask good questions and make great plans, avoiding a lot of nonsense that will otherwise waste your time. That doesn't mean you won't make mistakes, but I can help you avoid some of the bunny trails and pitfalls that come with a lot of business advice. I'll offer 15 years of experience consulting for large and small organizations across industries on how to create stand out organizations. As much as I've learned what to do, I've learned what to avoid in equal measure. I can offer you both and spare you frustration.

This book will help you to (1) clarify your intentions by focusing on the right things and asking good questions (assisting in part by pointing out industry nonsense I believe you can dismiss), (2) focus attention in the right places (again, dismissing distracting trends and rubbish), and (3) share wisdom from my years working with organizations who are great, and those who would like to be great. My hope is that you will create magic for yourself and others in your organization, and that the magic will lead your organization to success in ways that are unique and authentic to your purpose.

There are untold volumes of advice on how to have a successful organization, be a great employer, and reach fame and fortune. Organizational leaders constantly seek new methods of reaching these goals by attending conferences and webinars, reading books and keeping up on articles online. But most of this advice is closer to marketing than wisdom, and more trendy than timeless. When leaders get wrapped up in the newest buzz words and trends, it is almost always to the detriment of their organizations.

There are a few reasons why chasing after "what's new" is so harmful. First, when leadership asks their reports to implement something, whether the directive is to "improve employee engagement" or "introduce wellness programs," it is often unclear what this means. A lack of clarity is endemic to people practices in business. Someone somewhere gives a great presentation showing the amazing impact of improving employee engagement, and the next thing you know, everyone has to scramble to meet new goals without knowing how, or even exactly what it all means. This wastes employee time and frustrates everyone.

Another way things go wrong has to do with the pace of change. Every business in every industry is dealing with rapid change. Introducing additional, unnecessary change, often without a change management processes, fans the flames of chaos. The truth is that most people aren't amenable to change. It's easy for those who manage change relatively easily to forget the huge impact of even small changes on many people. Without knowing it, organizations add enormous amounts of stress in well-meaning attempts to make things better.

I've spent 15 years helping organizations to be great employers, and in the process have come head to head with many iterations of advice on perennial topics like leadership and employee satisfaction. I have helped employers sort their way through the wellness mania, employee engagement challenges, the culture craze, and a lot of confusion about "generations" among other things.

In this volume I provide a practical approach to important topics for leaders in business, showing how to cut through the bull and be an authentically great employer. I promise to save you and your employees a lot of time and heartache, and provide some relief from the swirling nonsense that embattles business leaders everywhere.

You will find a theme here that goes back to some very foundational matters—the "required skills and tools with which to win." The more of these we're able to gather, and the more we can promote in our employees, the better our outcomes will be. These skills and tools are not elaborate paradigms of organizational development, or recipes for a great culture. They are nothing like much of the leadership advice found in airport business books. The foundations for our success are all about our ability to know and manage ourselves, to relate well with others, and to ask good questions. Right now organizations are talking about the importance of Growth Mindset, Psychological Safety, Resilience, Agility, Inclusion, Burnout, and so on. The words will change over time, but the needs they represent will not. It's important to understand that what's underpinning them all are basic human qualities that we can all improve in ourselves and which are not only teachable, but can be encouraged in the social settings that are our organizations.

For example, it's critical that we all learn strategies to manage stress. This may mean identifying dysfunctional ways we react to stress (anger, eating, insomnia, shutdown, etc.) and replacing them with healthier responses. Similarly, we should identify patterns in our thinking that don't serve us well. Jan Bruce and Andrew Shatte, founders of the resilience building platform meQuilibrium, call these "icebergs" as habitual responses to certain types of situations which are often not appropriate or useful. When we learn our patterns, we can identify flaws in our thinking and subsequently move toward clearer thinking and better coping.

We can also improve our emotional intelligence and make the world feel safer and more comfortable for ourselves and others. For instance, foreseeing that some feedback you need to provide may make the recipient feel threatened, and using techniques to mitigate the perception of threat can completely change an interaction, a meeting, a project, and ultimately a workplace culture. Creating a safe, inclusive culture is impossible when members of the organization lack empathy, listening skills, and are too afraid to engage in dialogue.

Think for a moment about someone with whom you love to work—maybe a favorite colleague or a role model in your working life. Do they listen well? Are they empathetic? Do they manage their stress well? Have a sense of humor? Are they confident and grounded in a way that seems to allow them great ideas and insights? Do they display openness and authenticity in their work and interactions with others?

When we identify successful, happy people at work, it's more likely to be because they exhibit a strong set of social and emotional skills than because of any technical skills they possess.

Bring your sense of humor, your genuine purpose, an open mind, and your unique collection of skills and weaknesses to the chapters that follow. Ask the questions provided, and add your own.

CHAPTER 1

On Questions and Answers

On Questions

"Good questions, generously posed, seriously held, are powerful things."
Krista Tippet (2016, p. 108)

As a social scientist, I ask questions for a living. There's no better way to understand what your organization needs than to ask good questions and listen well to the answers. Great innovations begin with great questions. Great communication is at the core of organizational success.

Unfortunately, questioning isn't a part of the DNA of many organizations. Perhaps there's an unspoken understanding that questioning shows a lack of trust, is disrespectful, or reveals our ignorance when we ask. This is a detriment to us, and results in situations where large, angry elephants can stand on conference tables, unacknowledged.

One of the best things you can learn to do is to get comfortable asking questions. It requires putting yourself in a very open frame of mind, because if you have a judgment in your head, or think you know the answer, it will show when you ask the question. Practice asking neutrally phrased questions with a very open mind, with palpable curiosity. Done well, you can ask even very sensitive questions this way.

In one of my consulting jobs for a large organization who was trying to figure out how to support the childcare needs of their employees, I understood that a substantial proportion of the workforce were Mormon. I needed to know whether this meant that these employees tended to have larger families than the average American employee because I had to help determine what size their child care center should be. The organization didn't track these data, so I didn't know if this was my uninformed, biased perception, or whether it was a reality. The HR leadership asked me not to talk about it as I conducted interviews with the corporate leaders. My hands were tied. For the first few interviews nobody said the words "Mormon" or "LDS" (Latter Day Saints). Finally, in interview four, the gentleman I was interviewing mentioned the Church and I took the opening. He was very forthcoming and confirmed that in their population, LDS families tended to be large (he had something like seven children) and that there was more likely to be a stay-at-home mother in these families. In a later step in the consulting process I was able to confirm quantitatively that people working there had a higher than average number of children. This organization's reluctance to talk about the Mormon elephant in the room could have derailed our efforts to understand the needs of those employees if I hadn't been able to find an acceptable opportunity to get the information I needed.

I've seen it again and again that organizational history or ethos creates a fear or reluctance around certain issues. Coming in as an outsider, I'm often able to break through that because I don't have a horse in the race. There have also been times when I've had to do this in my own organization, and practice has allowed me to do so. If it's too scary to ask, you won't have the openness and confidence to pull it off and you'll come up against barriers. So I encourage you to practice on little things, because there will come a day when you need to ask a question that involves a sacred cow. Chances are that most people will be relieved that someone finally asked, but often there are some players who feel threatened and you must be the soul of authenticity and nonjudgment to pull it off.

Your organization is entirely unique. In 15 years of consulting I've learned to see some patterns, but each organization I enter has a different combination of key characteristics, resulting in an entirely one-of-a-kind outcome. Each organization is an amalgamation of its industry, region, urban or rural location, demographic profile, history, and so on. For that reason, no book of advice on how to make your organization great will be able to stand alone as a map for your journey. The best approach is to have clarity on the various relevant constructs (engagement, culture, etc.), and know how to ask questions that will help you chart your course.

To that end, this book is a guide to the various concepts relevant to being a great employer. It also provides questions to help you hone in on how these constructs apply in your organization. The answer to how to be a great employer is incredibly specific. In my work it's common for clients to ask "so what's new in cutting-edge people practice? What are other organizations doing that's cool?" And I always say "we need to focus on what makes sense for your needs. The cool things other organizations are doing aren't necessarily relevant to you."

The tendency to follow every workplace trend is worse than lemmings following one another off cliffs, it's more like dogs following lemmings off cliffs. Dogs should not worry about what lemmings are doing and vice versa.

Use the questions in this book to determine what kind of creature your organization is, what kind of care and feeding it needs, and to develop a unique approach to making it a great place to work and a successful business.

Each chapter to follow discusses an important construct and provides three sets of questions: One to ask yourself, another to ask leaders in your organization, and a third to use when surveying the workforce. Remember that how you ask the question has enormous influence on the answers you'll receive. Ask with generosity of heart, and without expectations about what the answers will, or should be.

On Answers

What will you do with all the answers you get? Answers to the questions you ask yourself will inform your next steps. You may or may not need to speak with leaders on any given topic, and you may or may not need to reach out to the workforce. You may find that upon answering the questions for yourself, you want to discuss them with a colleague, or do some further research on the topic. The questions you ask yourself will inevitably lead to more questions, and you will move more deeply into the issues that matter most for your organization.

One of the best pieces of advice I've gotten regarding questions is to allow myself to live inside them for a while. We've been taught to answer questions quickly, but often it's better not to. When you live inside a question, it begins to open up for you, showing more facets and perspectives than you recognized on first glance. Give yourself time to "sleep on it" a few times, and take advantage of the processing that happens over a matter of days. You will come to understand the question differently, gain patience in the process of answering, and ultimately come to richer, more useful answers.

Answers to the questions you ask leaders in your organization will also inform your next steps. Ideally, they will also open a dialogue about important issues. You will choose carefully which topics to take to leaders, and those choices may flag the need for change or reconsideration. This step should only come after a long, reflective period in the "questions you ask yourself" phase. There are only so many aspects of the organization you can address at one time, so make sure that when you take questions to your leaders you are presenting the topics you want to prioritize and opening a conversation. It's likely you'll ask questions your leaders have never considered before, so not only should you allow ample time for thought in the moment you ask the questions, you should also find ways to open doors to get each person's thoughts later on. Schedule a follow-up meeting, send a thank you note suggesting that you'd welcome any follow-up if they have further thoughts, include leaders in next-steps meetings, as appropriate, to chime in with ideas.

When you speak with leaders you'll encounter some enthusiasm and some resistance. Make careful note of where you see each, and seek to understand where they come from. Is the enthusiasm coming because the leader sees hope that your efforts will improve recruitment in a tight labor market? Do they hope for an innovative program that might garner positive media attention? Does resistance stem from feeling unprepared to consider a tough issue? Are there territorial issues that cause resistance to certain directions? Do leaders fear that the next step is to ask for a large investment in programs?

Negative or resistant feedback is at least as important as positive feedback. Never dismiss a naysayer. Figure out where that person is coming from and assume they have a valid point you need to consider. If they do, then don't hesitate to explore that concern thoroughly, even if it would be easier to ignore it. If their point doesn't appear valid even with further exploration, think about ways you can diplomatically present evidence that the danger they fear is a false one, or to reassure them that no decisions are being made yet and you will continue to seek their input and perspective.

Answers to the questions you ask employees are golden and can be used to respond to hesitant leaders. Just be sure to have buy-in before surveying the workforce and proceed with diplomacy when you need to provide evidence that refutes a leader's strongly held viewpoint.

While employee response rates to satisfaction surveys, engagement surveys, and the like are often in the 20 to 30 percent range, it is possible to get above 50 percent with an anonymous survey and higher with the one that is not. When surveys are identified (not anonymous) you have the ability to pinpoint areas of the company where response rates are low and push those employees to respond. For the most part, I prefer using anonymous surveys, however. You are looking for as much honesty as possible, and in most organizations, there is at least a little distrust about what will happen with the data. Employees especially fear revealing that they don't like their supervisor, that their productivity has been low, that they don't trust the organization's leadership, and so on. To further protect identity, demographic questions identifying race, gender, sexual preference, and so on should always be optional or have a "prefer not to answer" option. Do not read anything into the meaning of opting not to answer. I once saw a consulting firm categorize all the individuals who didn't answer the gender question as transgender, those who didn't answer race, as people of color, and those who didn't answer the sexual preference question as gay or bisexual. When they did that, they found that these "underrepresented" employees in the organization were less satisfied with the workplace than their counterparts in dominant groups. I suspected, however, that people were not answering those questions *because* they were dissatisfied employees and they didn't want to be identified. We went back to the data with the hypothesis that individuals who didn't answer one of those demographic questions didn't answer several. We supported our hypothesis and showed that nonanswers did not indicate membership in a minority category, unless we want to suppose that people who were minorities in race were consistently also minorities in sexual preference and gender identification. No, people who are unhappy don't want to reveal their details for fear of being found out. Those same people will skip the age question, a location question, and so on. So be careful reading into these things and when you want to understand the experience of your gay employees, look only at those who identify themselves that way.

While methodology regarding survey responses is beyond the scope of this book, I can offer a few guiding thoughts for best practices.

1. Where appropriate, customize the questions provided with your company's name and the correct way to refer to employees at your organization (associates, team members, etc.).

2. Make sure the answer scale matches the questions. I generally provide agree-scale questions, sometimes frequency scales. You may have taken surveys where you're asked a question but the answers don't make sense. Be careful to avoid this.

3. Pay attention when items that are answered in the reverse of the majority of items. For example, if you have agree scales with "strongly agree" on the right, coded "5" in the data, and most of your questions suggest a positive outcome when people agree (e.g., "I consider my company a great place to work"), then be careful with the questions that are in the reverse (e.g., I don't feel safe telling the truth when I miss work for personal reasons). I have noted which these are, but you will need to recode questions like this in the final dataset so that high scores are desirable outcomes and low scores are undesirable. This is especially important when you're adding items together in scales. Do not, however, seek to make sure everything is worded in the same direction in order to avoid having to recode. That will constrain your ability to ask questions in intuitive ways and will encourage respondents to get into automatic mode when answering.

4. Scales are useful for representing constructs with various aspects which can't all be represented well in one question. For example, when asking about financial well-being, you'll ask about both short-term and long-term finances, but to understand the whole of financial wellness, you may want add them together. When creating scales, it's important to make sure all items are coded in the same direction (see above), and test for scale reliability.

CHAPTER 2

Community

A great organization shares a lot in common with a great community.

Imagine an ideal community. It may be large or small, located anywhere—someplace you would like to live, or at least spend some time. Your community is filled with kind, welcoming people. They work and play well together, minimize in-fighting and competition, and see the best in one another. Maybe this community has a purpose or purposes such as tending bees and producing honey, or researching medical treatments. Whatever purpose, people are interested in their work, are eager to both teach and learn, and are collaborative in style.

In community, certain resources are shared, such as land, food, and knowledge. There are systems in place to nurse and nurture those in need—the very young, sick, and elderly. There are ways of transmitting knowledge across generations—through schools, or apprenticeships. A thriving community will have good communication and allow for self-expression. People feel safe there. The community draws out the willing contributions of members, and respects their need for solitude. An open-hearted community will allow for variation in how quickly members learn and mature, it will allow likes and dislikes and personal differences without judgment. For most people, specific qualities of the people in their ideal community are not important—qualities like physical characteristics, personal histories, or gender. As long as the people are kind, respectful, interesting, good communicators, and fun to be around.

How the life of the community is organized can vary. Perhaps there is one leader, or 50. Maybe people live in nuclear family units, or extended families, or in groups by interest or vocation. In a large community, there will always be subgroups of some kind, and how those groups function will influence the health of the whole, just as the well-being of each individual member influences the group.

An ideal community such as this can and should inspire the community we create at work. We don't live at work, but we do spend most of our waking hours working. Family aren't usually directly involved, but the great work communities I've seen do talk about their families and share support, parenting advice, funny stories, or whatever colors their days inside and outside of work.

Keep a vision of an ideal community in mind as you think about your workplace. A positive social community is at least as important as functional technology, a strong supply chain, or great marketing. In fact, studies have shown that sociability is positively related to productivity in the workplace. People who socialize at work have higher job satisfaction, and are more engaged (Karim et al. 2014, Gallup 2017, Riordan 2013). It's natural that having friends at work makes the day more fun, but it also enhances the quality of our work because our communication is better, we have higher levels of trust and cooperation, and we are more invested in creating positive outcomes for everyone.

In order to pull this off, we need our community members/colleagues to have emotional intelligence, the ability to manage their stress, willingness to change, resilience, and other foundational attributes which we'll discuss throughout this book.

Community Versus Culture

What I have described above is community, as distinct from culture. Corporations talk a lot about culture, but often they're actually referring to community. The following chapter will be dedicated to the concept of culture, but for now, I'd like to disentangle that from community.

When I walk into a new organization at the beginning of a consulting study, I absorb an enormous amount of information about the place in just the first few minutes. The important things I notice are markers of community. Do people make eye contact with me, a stranger in the building? Do people interact with one another in the hallways? When I arrive at my meeting, are participants chatting? If so, is it about work, or perhaps also about the weekend, family, and hobbies? I notice whether everyone sits at the table, who sits where and whether there is some negotiation or predetermined expectations about how that works. During the meeting, I notice whether meeting leaders intentionally create opportunities for shyer or younger members to give input. I notice how individuals respond to one another and the level of collaboration in the room. These things are all indicators of how this group works as a community.

Culture is a different layer—a more specific one, and not actually a solution for most of the issues organizations really face. In order to work from problem to solution, rather than the reverse, I've listed out some of the specific problems that organizations solve to. While this list can't possibly contain all the problems leaders seek to solve, it is a pretty comprehensive collection of the most common issues I see.

We want people to want to work here.
We want people to like working here and stay.
We want people be productive at work.
We want people to be creative and innovative.
We want to have great communication.
We want to reduce internal competition and in-fighting.
We want a strong talent pipeline for future leaders.

All of these goals share common solutions: a workplace with a strong community of people with the social and emotional skills to work together well.

It's clear that people are increasingly looking to work as a source of support. This is both because geographic mobility has reduced the probability that people have proximate family/long-time friends, and because we spend increasing amounts of time at work. In married couples, both spouses are often in the workforce, which adds to the shift of emphasis in our lives from neighborhood community to work community.

Look at the issues in the list above and try to find one that isn't solved by having the kind of community described at the beginning of this chapter. That is a community where people have the foundational skills needed to be:

Welcoming
Cooperative and collaborative
Purposeful

Nurturing

Empathetic

Open to differences

Able to manage in times of stress

Virtual Work

A special case concerning community at work is that of virtual employees. Having been one myself for 15 years, I am fascinated, when I spend a few days at the office, how much relationship building takes place and the level of intimacy that's built between co-workers working proximally. The last time I was at the office I learned about co-workers' parents, their planned dates, the outfits for those dates, and the state of someone's closet and of someone else's refrigerator. The sharing of those small, day-to-day life details, piled one upon the next almost every day for years creates remarkable relationships. Neither all good nor all bad, I think it's important to recognize that we may know our co-workers better than anyone else outside our families. Leaders concerned with people dynamics should think deeply about this because it helps us understand the gravity of turnover, and even of incidents of injured morale for one or more members of the community. We should also think about how the lack of these daily interactions impacts virtual employees.

Virtual work is increasingly popular both as a way to reduce costs for employers and to provide flexibility for employees. Like many virtual workers, I find it's great for productivity, but I sometimes miss the face-to-face interaction with colleagues.

Studies have shown that employees working from home are more productive than their counterparts in the office. In fact, a recent study by Nicholas Bloom at Stanford showed that telecommuters were not only significantly more productive, but their turnover was 50 percent lower, and they took fewer sick days (Mautz 2018). Saving time by not commuting, reducing hallway conversations, and taking shorter lunches gives us more time in the day. Even if we are juggling kids to and from school, making ourselves available for the school performance, and prepping dinner while listening to a conference call, our productivity is higher. We can fold laundry while listening to a call or webinar, we can get out and walk the dog to get a bit of fresh air and revitalize our brains. We're there for the cable guy, a sick kid, or a delivery.

The flip said of telecommuting is that it can be lonely. It's harder to build strong relationships with co-workers, and you miss out on the joys of working truly together on a project. When I was a professor, virtual learning was just starting to take off and I didn't want to participate because it was so important to me to crouch down next to a student's desk and look at their work with them. I wanted to see the expressions on their faces as I taught, and read their body language. I feel much the same way about work. I'm amazed how much I accomplish on the days when I'm at our corporate office. Being able to read the people in the room during a meeting makes a world of difference. As I mentioned earlier, being social at work has positive outcomes including higher productivity and job satisfaction, greater trust and cooperation, and lower turnover.

Many virtual workers perceive disadvantages in terms of advancement opportunities. This can be a matter of simply not having the same level of noticeable presence and networking opportunities, or it can be related to the fact that some supervisory roles need a physical office presence to be most effective. There are plenty of highly successful virtual managers, but it depends on the kind of work they're doing. In consulting and research, I've found managing and being managed virtually works well; however, my architecture firm client would maintain that it's critical to be in the same room with a team working on drawings.

Virtual work isn't an all-or-nothing proposition. Some people work from home a day or more per week, but also have a regular office presence. In small organizations these arrangements are often informal, but in larger organizations it can be good to have guidelines for managers about how work-from-home decisions are made. Considerations often include the type of role the employee plays, the length of their commute, and personal preferences. Family caregiving responsibilities can also play a role. Because these decisions can get complicated and can have optics of being unfair, it's helpful for more formal organizations to create guidelines to the degree that they can and always communicate clearly about why decisions are made. It is more often the decisions that aren't explained that cause resentment. Colleagues are truly able to understand special arrangements when someone has an elder care responsibility, a horrible commute, or a new puppy. Sometimes arrangements change for the short term, sometimes for longer, but transparency should be the default whenever it doesn't violate privacy.

How can we build stronger relationships, have more social bonding, and create strong community when working virtually? Technology companies like Slack, Facebook, and Google all have apps designed to facilitate workplace communication across distance. The ability to chat easily, organize conversations, and share living documents help to connect people and get the work done. Video conferencing tools put a face to the words of our colleagues and can help connect us. They can also show us how bored our colleagues are, as well as what they're eating for lunch. Screen sharing and the ability to "remote" into one another's computers are also effective ways to interact and lend assistance.

It's a good investment to bring virtual workers and teams together regularly. I once worked with an organization where some teams were only funded to meet once per year, and some virtual employees had never met another single employee of their company. It's tough to build trust and engagement under those circumstances.

Whether we're working together in an office or across the world from one another, soft skills and emotional intelligence are critical. While some personalities on a team will "click" easily, others will be fraught with prickles. Working across uncomfortable relationships requires confidence, empathy, and an awareness that effort is required. When I was younger I took each relationship as it came, not realizing that I had the ability to make the poor ones better. Now I put in effort, often relying on my understanding of how to make communication and relationships feel safe. I have to remind myself constantly to think about how the other person may be threatened by my direct communication style, to understand that they may be in defense mode when I don't realize it, and to find ways to show my appreciation for their contributions. We can make others feel safe by disarming tense situations with authenticity and humor, by showing how much we value others as people, and by being transparent in our own work lives. A colleague respected for his data prowess once said to me "I'm the King of Errors." Forever after, I felt comfortable with my mistakes and flaws and we created a safe and highly functional cross-check for each other to catch mistakes.

Humans are social animals. Our survival depends upon one another. So how do we help build critical and foundational capacities in workplaces? That is the topic of this book. I will present answers in the following chapters under the headings of common organizational concepts, and in the process I will clean and clarify those concepts, reducing them to what is essential for your efforts and discarding the parts that confuse and waste time and energy. Every chapter in this book is relevant to the topic of community and points back to the importance of key competencies.

Questions to Ask Yourself

1. What would my ideal community look like?
2. What would life be like if my workplace was that ideal community?
3. What social and emotional capacities would people in my ideal community have?
4. What workplace experiences are most unlike my ideal community?
5. What aspects of my ideal community are already in place at work?
6. Are there things about the physical setup of work that create opportunities and challenges for community?
7. How are coffee and social areas arranged—do they encourage work groups to stick together or to mingle? How well utilized are they?
8. Are there ways in which our organizational chart creates opportunities and challenges for community?
9. What resources do we share within the work community and how does that create challenges and opportunities?
10. What are a couple of easy things we could do to improve the work community?
11. What could we do to improve individual social and emotional capacities?
12. What are the hardest/most intractable obstacles to reaching the ideal?
13. Do you prefer working out of the office or from home or an off-site location?
14. What are the advantages you see of each?
15. What do you believe are "good reasons" to work virtually?

16. If you work in the office, you ever find yourself doubting the commitment of colleagues you don't see at the office?
17. If you work virtually, do you ever feel like people doubt your commitment?
18. Have you seen yourself or others overlooked for promotions because of working remotely?

Questions to Ask Leaders in Your Organization

1. Do you think it's important for employees here to feel a sense of community at work?
2. (If yes) What do you think are important qualities of a work community?
3. What personal qualities do you think people need to have in order to function well in the work community?
4. Do you think there are ways that our org. chart and our physical setup make community difficult to achieve?
5. What would you like to see improved in terms of how employees here relate to one another?
6. What do you think would be the benefits of improving the level of social support/community among employees?
7. Do you see any potential downside to working toward the goals you've mentioned? (Fill in specific goals)
8. Who do you consider the responsible party or department for an initiative to meet these goals (be specific).
9. Do we have a policy or philosophy about which positions in our company can be virtual and which cannot?
10. How many fully virtual employees do we have?
11. What is our policy around part-time working from home?
12. What special efforts do we have in place to engage and connect virtual employees using technology?
13. Do we have guidelines on how often virtual employees should meet in person with their teams or spend time at headquarters?
14. Have we ever examined whether virtual employees receive the same advancement opportunities as office-based employees?

15. Do you think managers here are transparent about how work-arrangement decisions are made?

Questions for Surveying the Workforce

(Agree scale unless noted.) (R) is the marker for reverse coding

1. My colleagues at work are very supportive of me.
2. I feel a sense of community at work.
3. I want to have a sense of community at work.
4. I feel that my workplace could be more supportive (R).
5. The workplace setup makes it difficult to develop relationships with colleagues (R).
6. Co-workers tend to be competitive here (R).
7. I have at least one person at work I could turn to with a personal problem.
8. My manager fosters a sense of camaraderie in our team.
9. Power dynamics among groups make community difficult here (R).
10. My colleagues sometimes seem to lack the communication skills needed in order for things to go smoothly (R).
11. My colleagues regularly show support and empathy for one another.
12. People on my work team are good at managing the stress they feel.
13. When you need help with a family or personal matter, who do you turn to? (Check all that apply: family, friends, church or other community group, workplace or colleagues, neighbors).
14. *(multiple choice)* Is your primary working arrangement: (a) office or facility-based, (b) part-time from an off-site location like home, and (c) full-time virtual location?
15. My work location arrangement is productive for me.
16. My work location arrangement allows me to meet my work and non-work obligations.
17. Decisions about who works in the office and who works from home make sense to me.
18. Virtual workers are given the same respect as those who work in the office or on-site. (Include "don't know" option)

19. Virtual workers are given the same advancement opportunities as those who work in the office or on-site. (Include "don't know" option)

20. Virtual workers are well enabled with the technology they need to connect and collaborate. (Include "don't know" option)

CHAPTER 3

Culture

In Chapter 2 I described the difference between community and culture at work. While "great culture" has become a beacon for many leaders, I believe it's a bit of a siren. It promises that employees will want to work for your organization, love being there, and want to stay. However, without a great community, the promise of culture is empty at best. At worst, it is harmful.

In sociology and anthropology, culture is defined as a set of learned behaviors and values, as well as artifacts like art, music, food, tools, and so on. Some corporations mistake culture for some sort of holy grail and work on that level (the food, recreation, decor, etc.) rather than developing strong community. While we all want good food, and some people want ping-pong, too much attention to culture can be counterproductive for our goals.

"One culture," the mantra of cultural homogeneity touted by many organizations, is not only unrealistic, but undesirable. It does not make sense that subgroups within organizations should all look and feel the same. Leaders in different parts of organizations will have different styles. Offices in different parts of the world will have different ways of doing things, a different look and feel—appropriately so. Who wants to walk into an office in Tokyo and have it feel just like the office in New York? Apparently some leaders do, but the effort has to be forced, and the culture no longer resonates with the surroundings. The Shanghai office looks and feels different from Los Angeles. The finance department has different goals, leadership, and personalities than human resources. Having strong community in each subgroup, as well as across groups, should be a primary goal. But having "one culture" is an ideal we should dispense with.

"Yes," leaders say, but what if our "one culture is a positive culture? What if we emphasize health and the importance of family, and we have casual Friday?"

These are all positive things, but we don't want to define ourselves or our people around things that may make some feel excluded. If I work in a culture that defines itself around health, and I have severe health challenges, I may feel like I don't belong. Or, for example, not everyone has family, and, I hear from employees in family-oriented work cultures that they feel less valuable or excluded because they don't. Community connects to everyone in every circumstance without the added weight of defining certain lifestyles or characteristics as more desirable than others.

Another common mistake regarding culture is to look at examples like Google and infer that good culture is about workplace perks like indoor basketball courts, great food, and stylish decor. These aren't bad things to have, but they don't change important factors like how work community functions.

I've seen many organizations adopt the tagline "Culture is the way we do things around here." This is another mistake. Do you really want "a way" of doing things? Aren't most organizations desperate for innovation? New ways of thinking, new perspectives, and new contributions offer organizations' best chance for success in the midst of rapid change.

"Hire for fit" is a directive that has come out of the culture movement, and is another dangerous dictate. It too often results in more of the same, with managers giving preference to hires who look and act like them. "Hire for add" is a better approach.

From one side of their mouths, organizations have been saying "we want to be diverse and inclusive," and from the other side, "we want to have one culture." How, I ask you, can these two live together? How can we respect difference when we preach sameness?

I was in a conversation recently where an organization leader kept emphasizing the importance of leadership transmitting the company's culture. While leadership should live the values they believe in, no amount of trying to transmit it to others will be effective if the others don't ascribe to that culture and values. Employees aren't lemmings. If we want good culture, it has to come from the individuals involved. It can't be transmitted or imposed by leadership. Culture develops naturally as a result of the time, place, and people involved. If you have great community, culture will flourish and vary all over your organization. That should be celebrated.

So what can we gain from efforts around culture? If we go in the opposite direction from "one culture" and celebrate the authentic and organic development of multiple cultures within our organizations, we will likely further our goals for diversity, inclusion, and social justice. We can certainly enjoy introducing various aspects of physical culture—from food to decor, to recreation.

The culture trend has not been all bad. Acknowledging that people need social and recreational outlets during the day is a positive development (see discussion of energy in Chapter 5). The culture movement also brought attention to the need for good food and pleasant surroundings at work. It cast a suspicious eye at office arrangements that create barriers rather than encouraging collaboration. And yet, studies show that when we open up the floor plan too much, distraction erodes productivity. Look for a balance between private, quiet work spaces and spaces designed to facilitate collaboration. Trying to have all spaces be a combination of these two results in a failure of both.

Questions to Ask Yourself

1. What statements does my organization make about our culture?
2. What goals or directives have been stated?
3. Have our culture people sat down to discuss things with our diversity people?
4. Have we become distracted by managing decor, recreation, and food to the exclusion of community?

Questions to Ask Leaders in Your Organization

1. How do you think about culture at our organization?
2. Do you believe we should strive to have a culture that looks and feels the same companywide?
3. If you could change something about our culture, what would it be?
4. Do you think culture should be defined by leaders, grown from the workforce, or a combination?

5. How has attention to culture at our organization improved the work experience for employees?

Questions for Surveying the Workforce

(Agree scale unless noted.) (R) is the marker for reverse coding

1. My organization has a culture I enjoy.
2. The culture in my organization feels very similar across divisions and locations (as applicable).
3. The culture here makes sense given the kind of work my department does.
4. The way our leaders talk about our culture is consistent with how I experience it.
5. I like the culture here more than I have at other places I've worked (provide N/A option).
6. This organization has spent put too much effort into superficial culture without addressing underlying problems (R).

CHAPTER 4

Well-Being

Well-being is the primary goal of any community for itself and its members. A state of well-being is one in which we function well in all areas of our lives. This doesn't mean that every aspect of our organization or of each individual is always thriving. We all face challenges, which are essential to our growth and learning.

The workplace focus on employee well-being developed out of the "wellness" craze, which was primarily focused on physical health. As it turned out, wellness programming wasn't the panacea employers were hoping it would be. In fact, a 2018 study showed that when subjected to a randomized control trial, wellness programs showed no effect on health care spending, employee exercise, or intent to stay with the organization (Jones et al. 2018). Employee well-being entered the picture because a larger view was needed.

The well-being lens approaches employees as whole people. In order to embrace it as a goal in the corporate world, leaders had to set aside the old management idea that "what happens outside the office walls is none of our business," and recognize that people don't leave their lives at home when they come to work. If someone is distracted because their mother is ill, because they don't feel good about their child care provider, because their finances are a mess, or because their marriage in ruin, they will not be able to perform well at work. Making that case (which is incredibly intuitive, and yet was hard won in the corporate world) opened the door for supporting employees in completely new ways.

Today, great organizations make efforts to recognize the importance of people's lives outside of work. They recognize that most people have several priorities in their lives which rank above work, and that this isn't a bad thing. For the sake of society, we want people to prioritize caregiving for children and elders, having personal stability, having meaningful pursuits outside of work, and being healthy. Great employers seek ways to provide supports to help people with these goals and they see great pay-off in employee engagement and loyalty. These employers build healthy work communities by allowing all the aspects of life in community to be acknowledged, and by recognizing the fundamental capabilities people need in order to function well in society.

Maslow's Hierarchy and Well-Being

Maslow's hierarchy of needs was an important contribution to our under-standing of well-being because he pointed to the foundational importance of certain aspects of our experience. However, it's best to view the hierarchy with a flexible mind. People in situations where their basic needs are not being met have often been able to achieve higher states of function, includ-ing self-actualization, the pinnacle of the pyramid. Still, the model is instruc-tive in the sense that it points to our general ability to proceed from one level of well-being to the next most easily when we have a strong foundation.

One of the problems with the wellness craze was that there was an implicit expectation that employees would jump at the chance to improve their wellness and their success would lead to better outcomes for them personally and for the company as a whole (the health insurance premiums most explicitly). What happened was that individuals who were ready to take the next step in improving their health enrolled in these programs, and many had good outcomes. However, once the first cohort completed the programs, enrollment dropped off. Organizations weren't able to get people to participate, or when they did, their outcomes weren't as impres-sive. Beyond that first "ready" cohort were people who had more immediate stresses in their lives which meant that it wasn't the best time to quit smoking, lose weight, start and maintain an exercise program, and so on. While those activities would doubtless help these individuals, it is sometimes unrealistic to expect big changes when there are other stresses looming. For example, if someone is in deep financial trouble, their marriage is falling apart or their teenager is getting in trouble, it may not be the best time to lose weight. The immediate problems causing high levels of stress need to be resolved first.

What I just said inverts Maslow's hierarchy a bit. He placed physio-logical needs at the very base, and security and family higher up. How-ever, like I said, we need to be flexible. The basic physiological needs he was pointing to were things like food, shelter, and air—certainly prereq-uisites. And still the model helps us because it cues us to think about an "order of operations" in our lives. Immediate life stresses need to be solved prior to the next goal.

People do want to improve their lives, so when we consider all aspects of life in which they may need support, we can facilitate the journey. When finances are stabilized and family issues are improving, an individ-ual can take a breath and focus on the next goal—be that advancement at work or losing weight.

Whether we're looking at Maslow's hierarchy of needs, or any model of well-being, it's helpful to consider the role of resilience and energy, which are the topic of the next chapter. We should assume that at any given moment, some area of life will experience challenges. Stasis simply isn't a reality during human life, nor the life of an organization. Chal-lenges are our opportunities to grow and learn. When some aspect of our experience is challenged, it doesn't mean that the whole pyramid has to tumble. Even if a foundational building block is weakened, the structure can be shored up. It is resilience that allows us to manage through diffi-culties, and the more energy we have, the better.

Models of Well-Being

There are a number of well-being models in the corporate consulting marketplace, most of which will define the aspects of well-being and tell you what percent of overall well-being comes from each compo-nent. However, I see this as a false imposition. I've seen all variation in what makes up well-being for the people of various organizations. In the health care industry, physical health tends to be a more important factor than in other industries. In higher education, job satisfaction is particularly important. And of course, this variation extends to indi-viduals, and changes over the life course. It may be that family and per-sonal life is most important during someone's 30s and 40s, and health becomes paramount later in life. For some individuals, spirituality is a very large piece of their well-being, while others don't consider it at all. Thinking about well-being is more specific than a general model implies.

Life Stages

Life stage plays a role in understanding variance in what makes up well-being for individuals. In very general terms, our youngest employees tend to be focused on education, career growth, and creating financial sustainability. The next life stage during their careers is often an increased focus on familial responsibilities as families are started and life complicates in that way. As employees age out of the intense child-rearing years, they may shift focus to caring for elder relatives. Personal health concerns and career development wax and wane over the course of our careers, as do financial concerns. When you consider your organization, take a look at the age and gender profiles of your workforce, and subareas of your workforce. This will suggest areas of inquiry regarding what those employees may need to support their well-being.

The Whole Self at Work

Considering holistic well-being has helped us to think about the whole person at work in multiple ways. In addition to considering the various aspects of well-being mentioned above, we're learning to think about whether people feel comfortable bringing important parts of their identities to work. If step one is feeling comfortable acknowledging that our financial well-being, our relationships, and our health impact us at work, step two is thinking about whether people are able to be themselves. When we're able to be fully ourselves in our community, we feel safe, welcomed, and able to make our best contributions, which include bringing our unique perspectives to the table. Does it feel okay to be gay, Mormon, Indian, in a wheelchair, the parent of a special-needs child? Do people know these things about one another? It's okay if private-leaning people don't want to share, but to the degree that our identities inform our lives, and to the degree that we want their importance acknowledged, our workplace communities should welcome them. Characteristics that cannot be hidden are, of course, of prime concern, and we need to monitor the degree to which our community welcomes and supports the full spectrum of humanity. I will discuss this more in the chapter on diversity and inclusion in the workplace.

How to Apply the Well-Being Paradigm in Your Workplace

Think of well-being as a paradigm that helps us to consider all aspects of the kinds of challenges people face, and to think about how people thrive.

Train managers to keep the whole picture of their people in mind, and to approach their employees with compassion and understanding when issues arise. In an ideal community, members are not shocked when challenges enter the lives of their friends. They know that this is natural part of life and compassion and support are called for. Unfortunately, the old ethos of (pretending to) keep "life" separate from work has meant that it is frowned upon for people to have these struggles, or it feels that way because they aren't allowed to be whole people at work, so they hide their problems, fib about why they need to leave early, and hide to make a phone call to try to arrange a nurse for mom.

Telling people to keep their personal problems out of the office simply doesn't work, so instead, good employers offer help in the form of employee assistance programs, child and elder care resources, financial counseling, wellness programs, and employee support groups. Add flexible scheduling (to the extent possible), manager training to improve emotional intelligence and explicitly give managers permission to work in support of people's challenges. Provide programs that help everyone learn to manage stress and create balance in their lives.

There should be a visible companywide willingness to acknowledge that we all have multiple priorities and we don't have to hide them. I have seen managers post out-of-office replies that tell the truth: "I'm at my son's school play this afternoon, I'll reach out to you when I get back" or "I'm traveling to visit colleges with my daughter, if you need immediate help, please call so-and-so." That kind of honest transparency speaks volumes and gives everyone permission to admit that they have priorities outside of work. Those are the organizations where we all want to work and have community.

Questions to Ask Yourself

1. Does your organization have a high proportion of younger or older employees? If so, what might that tell you about the life-stage needs of your population?
2. Is there something specific to your industry that might reveal the priorities of the people there?
3. Are people comfortable being honest when they have to miss work for personal reasons?
4. Do your employees know important things about one another as people? Hobbies, spouse and children's names, and so on?
5. Are people comfortable sharing important parts of their identity that have historically been hidden, downplayed, or caused discrimination in the workplace?
6. Does your organization offer supportive programs and benefits for physical, emotional, and financial well-being? Do you offer resources for family care?

Questions to Ask Leaders in Your Organization

1. To what degree do you believe that supporting the challenges employees face outside of work helps us to be a better employer?
2. Are there certain areas of employees' lives where you think our company should offer supportive programs or benefits?
3. Are there any areas of employees' lives where you think the company should not consider providing supports?
4. Given the profile of employees here, what do you expect are common challenges they face in their lives?
5. What aspects of where our office is (locations are) create challenges for people?
6. Do you foresee any changes to our employees' needs based on demographic changes in our workforce?
7. Are you aware of any patterns in voluntary turnover that we may be able to impact by providing support?
8. What do you consider the main reasons people want to work here?

9. Setting cost and other practical matters aside, what do you wish our company could do to support employees? (Possibly probe areas of education and career development, health, financial well-being, family well-being, and resilience)

Questions for Surveying the Workforce

Some of the questions that make sense here will be presented in chapters to follow. For example, resilience and energy are important to well-being, and specific questions on those topics are provided in the chapter to follow. Employee engagement questions are in that chapter, and so on. The questions below are arranged in groups which can be used to create scales representing the different areas of well-being. Items should be tested for cohesion using factor analysis and reliability testing. Items should be on an agreement scale (typically five points), unless otherwise noted. Remember that you may have to reverse the coding of some items in scales (when the questions are posed in the negative versus positive). Those items are marked with an (R).

Financial Well-Being

1. I have confidence in my ability to create a budget for myself/my family.
2. I have confidence in my ability to meet my financial obligations each month.
3. My retirement savings plan is on track.
4. I feel confident about my ability to pay for my education/repay education loans (include N/A option).
5. I have confidence in my ability to save for my children's education (include N/A option).
6. If I/my family had a $5,000 emergency, I'm confident I'd be able to manage.
7. I have a good sense of how much I can spend on non-necessities each month.
8. I have the financial ability to take at least a modest vacation each year.

Physical Wellness

1. I feel that my current weight is healthy.
2. I feel that my current eating habits are healthy.
3. I'm satisfied with the amount of exercise I get most weeks.
4. I am more than 10 pounds from being a healthy weight (R).
5. I have difficulty eating healthy meals when I'm at work (R).
6. I often skip meals or eat unhealthy things on the run (R) (note, this is an example of a double-barreled question, which is to say people could say yes to one part, but no to another. However, there are times (like this) when you can use them, as long as you don't care if agreement means one, the other, or both).
7. I have significant health issues that would likely improve if I took better care of myself (R).
8. My doctor has suggested I make lifestyle changes in order to improve my health (R).
9. I am affected by a chronic health condition (R).
10. Compared with others my age, I am very healthy.

Personal Life/Relationships

1. Overall, I'm satisfied with my personal life.
2. Overall, my personal relationships are good.
3. I feel able to give my family the attention they need (include N/A).
4. I have a supportive network of people who I can call on if I'm in need.
5. I have had a major stressful life even in the past year (R).
6. I am currently dealing with a very difficult situation in my personal/ family life (R).

CHAPTER 5

Mental and Behavioral Health

Organizations are increasingly recognizing the importance of supporting not just physical health, but mental and behavioral health as well. By emphasizing these aspects of health, not only can services be made available to struggling people, but issues that often snowball into larger problems are caught early. Ideally, employees have access to the resources and services they need to manage through difficulties in life and rebound before declining into depression, severe anxiety, substance abuse, or other unhealthy coping behaviors.

It's clear that comorbidity between mental and physical health issues is high, and while the direction of causality isn't always clear, better mental health improves physical health, and addressing the mental and emotional aspects of sickness is always important.

For example, obesity often presents along with mood disorders and physical ailments such as hypertension and ulcers.[1] It can be difficult to identify if one causal factor exists, but improvement on any one presenting issue helps to improve the entire cluster.

A large study in New Zealand examined the relationship between anxiety, depression, and bipolar disorder, and long-term physical health conditions. The study reported that having one of these mental disorders increased the odds of stroke, cardiovascular disease, chronic pain, arthritis, asthma, and high cholesterol.[2]

---

[1] Romain, A.J., J. Marleay, and A. Bailot. 2018. "Impact of Obesity and Mood Disorders on Physical Comorbidities, Psychological Well-Being, Health Behaviours and Use of Health Services." *Journal of Affective Disorders* 225, pp. 381–388.
[2] Lockett, H., A. Jury, C. Tuason, J. Lai, and D. Fergusson. 2018. "Comorbidities Between Mental and Physical Health Problems: An Analysis of the New Zealand Health Survey Data." https://psychology.org.nz/wp-content/uploads/NZJP-Vol-47-No-3-November-2018.pdf#page=5

In a study estimating the costs of modifiable health risks, which are often related to poor mental and behavioral health, researchers estimated that the additional annual medical expenditures for a worker with high blood pressure were 32 percent higher than for a worker without high blood pressure. Workers with high blood glucose were 32 percent more costly than were those at lower risk, and obese workers were 27 percent more costly than normal or overweight employees.

> Today, many employers are implementing health promotion programs that include regular behavioral and biometric screenings with the expectation that these initiatives will lead to cost savings. Achieving long-term behavior change and risk reduction in an employed population is, admittedly, difficult. Employers that succeed in doing so, however, may reap benefits from both lower medical spending and a more productive workforce.[3]

The comorbidity of mood disorders and substance abuse is widely acknowledged, but it may vary whether the substance use started as a form of medication (prescribed or self-medicated), or whether abuse of substances led to the mood disorder.

Whatever the case of causality, improving mental health is important to improving overall health. Mentally healthy people are better able to make positive lifestyle decisions, are more likely to adhere to doctors' instructions, and proceed with more optimism than those who are struggling with mental health issues.

Depression

Depression is a common mental health issue that affects millions of Americans. According to the National Institute of Mental Health, approximately seven percent of U.S. adults suffer a major depressive episode in a

---

[3]   Goetzel, R.Z., X. Pei., M.J. Tabrizi., R.M. Henke., N. Kowlessar., C.F. Nelson., and R.D. Metz. 2012. "Ten Modifiable Health Risk Factors Are Linked To More Than One-Fifth Of Employer-Employee Health Care Spending." *Health Affairs* 31, no. 11, ACOS, Medical Homes, Nursing, Costs and Quality.

given year. If you think about a work group or a meeting with 14 people in it, statistics predict that one has suffered serious depression in the past year, or someone is suffering now.[4]

When people are depressed, they work hard to conceal it. More than 70 percent of employees with mental illnesses hide their struggles from their managers and co-workers for a number of reasons, including fear of jeopardizing their job.[5]

The *Diagnostic and Statistical Manual of Mental Disorders* (DSM-IV), used by clinicians and psychiatrists to diagnose psychiatric illnesses, defines a major depressive episode as

A period of two weeks or longer during which there is either depressed mood or loss of interest or pleasure, and at least four other symptoms that reflect a change in functioning, such as problems with sleep, eating, energy, concentration, self-image or recurrent thoughts of death or suicide.[6]

Some of the common signs and symptoms of depression include:

- Persistent sad, anxious, or "empty" mood.
- Feelings of hopelessness, or pessimism.
- Irritability.
- Feelings of guilt, worthlessness, or helplessness.
- Loss of interest or pleasure in hobbies and activities.
- Decreased energy or fatigue.
- Moving or talking more slowly.
- Feeling restless or having trouble sitting still.

---

[4]   National Institute of Mental Health. February 2018.

[5]   Evans-Lacko, S., and M. Knapp. 2018. "Is Manager Support Related to Workplace Productivity for People with Depression: A Secondary Analysis of a Cross-Sectional Survey from 15 Countries." *BMJ Open* 8, no. 6, p. e021795. Published 2018 Jul 23. doi:10.1136/bmjopen-2018-021795. https://ncbi.nlm.nih.gov/pmc/articles/PMC6059307/

[6]   *Diagnostic and Statistical Manual of Mental Disorders: DSM-IV-TR*, American Psychiatric Association, 1994.

- Difficulty concentrating, remembering, or making decisions.
- Difficulty sleeping, early-morning awakening, or oversleeping.
- Appetite and/or weight changes.
- Thoughts of death or suicide, or suicide attempts.
- Aches or pains, headaches, cramps, or digestive problems without a clear physical cause.[7]

The Financial Cost of Depression

While the most important cost—the human cost—can't be quantified, the financial cost to employers related to depression can be estimated and includes avoidable absences, lost productivity due to presenteeism, and turnover.

Absenteeism and presenteeism alone were estimated to cost U.S. employers $43 billion in 2010.[8]

Foundational skills to support mental health can be taught, and depression risk can be measurably reduced. Employers can help manage depression risk by investing in resources to train employees to manage stress, improve emotional awareness, and care for their own mental health. This behavior also sends a strong message that mental health is important and that the employer is invested in supporting employees.

Anxiety

Twenty-four hour news cycles and traumatic world events appear to have increased anxiety for many people. Constant change at work and news of workplace violence also raises anxiety levels.

Anxiety disorders, including panic disorder with or without ago-raphobia, generalized anxiety disorder, social anxiety disorder, specific phobias, and separation anxiety disorder, are the most

---

[7]   National Institute of Mental Health. February 2018.

[8]   Greenberg, P.E., A.A. Fournier, T. Sisitsky, C.T. Pike, and R.C. Kessler. no date. "The Economic Burden of Adults with Major Depressive Disorder in the United States." https://pdfs.semanticscholar.org/2a0f/0218f857e39e2576a024e1 c484c9edc1a9e7.pdf

prevalent mental disorders and are associated with immense health care costs and a high burden of disease. According to large population-based surveys, up to 33.7 percent of the population are affected by an anxiety disorder during their lifetime.[9]

People with generalized anxiety disorder display excessive anxiety or worry, most days for at least 6 months, about a number of things such as personal health, work, social interactions, and everyday routine life circumstances. The fear and anxiety can cause significant problems in areas of their life, such as social interactions, school, and work.

Generalized anxiety disorder symptoms include:

- Feeling restless, wound-up, or on-edge
- Being easily fatigued
- Having difficulty concentrating; mind going blank
- Being irritable
- Having muscle tension
- Difficulty controlling feelings of worry
- Having sleep problems, such as difficulty falling or staying asleep, restlessness, or unsatisfying sleep[10]

Of course, a diagnosed anxiety disorder is just one extreme. The majority of people struggle with anxiety at some level, at some times in life. Learning to manage anxiety is an important life skill, and it can be taught through similar processes as teaching emption management and other self-regulation skills.

Anxiety plays out problematically and even dangerously in the workplace. When people are anxious, brain activity is centered in the primitive "fight or flight" areas of the brain, and individuals become reactive and defensive. It is damaging to work relationships, project collaboration, and the ability to manage change.

---

[9]   NCBI. https://ncbi.nlm.nih.gov/pmc/articles/PMC4610617/
[10]   National Institute of Mental Health. February 2018.

Individuals need to learn to manage their own anxiety at work, and also to recognize when others are suffering from anxiety and find ways to be supportive. Managers need training. Everyone needs training on the basics of how stress impacts us and what to do about it.

Substance Use Issues

About 1 in 20 people in the United States suffer from substance dependency including alcohol, prescription, and nonprescription drugs. While every situation is unique, there are some foundational skills that reduce the risk of addiction and, for those already addicted, improve the possibility of recovery. Among those key skills are stress management, emotional awareness, and pain management.

Employees who abuse prescription drugs are two-to-five times more likely to take unexcused absences, be late for work, be injured or violent at work, file workers' compensation claims, or quit or be fired within one year of employment, according to the National Safety Council.

The U.S. Department of Labor lists the following signs and symptoms frequently associated with substance abuse issues:

- Lowered productivity
- Increased absenteeism
- Inconsistent work quality
- Poor concentration
- Careless mistakes
- Needless risk taking
- Disregard for safety
- Errors in judgment

According to the National Safety Council, the annual cost associated with lost time, job turnover, and health care per 1,000 employees with substance use disorder in the manufacturing industry, for example, is $340,428. They estimate that each worker in recovery saves their employer $3,200 per year. [11]

---

[11] https://nsc.org/forms/substance-use-employer-calculator

There are many factors that lead people into the unfortunate position of becoming drug dependent. Three important ones are stress, mood disorder, and pain. When people learn to manage these experiences more effectively, they improve their ability to regain health and sobriety. We know that people are healthiest when they have good social connections in their lives, so we also need skills like empathy, positivity, and connection to other people and a greater good.

Researcher Johann Hari, in an exploration of the truth about addiction, asserts that physical chemical dependency does not explain addiction. Rather, life circumstance predicts whether someone who uses an opioid for pain, for example, will become addicted.

A core part of addiction is about not being able to bear to be present in your life.—Johann Hari[12]

Foundational life skills create a state of mental health and emotional awareness that allow individuals to be resilient to challenges and cope effectively without resorting to misuse of substances. Focusing on mental and emotional skill building supports people in their ability to address whatever is going on in their lives. Medical help can be necessary for serious addiction problems, but in all cases, the ability to manage stress and emotions is foundational.

Stress and Substance Use

A rising concern with employers, substance abuse, and specifically opioid addiction are dangerous and costly both in terms of dollars and human potential.

There is substantial literature on the significant association between acute and chronic stress and the motivation to abuse addictive substances.[13] Stress is a key risk factor in starting, maintaining, and relapsing into

---

[12]   Hari, J. no date. "TED Talk." https://ted.com/talks/johann_hari_everything_you_think_you_know_about_addiction_is_wrong/discussion#t-450576

[13]   Sinha, R. 2001. "How Does Stress Increase Risk of Drug Abuse and Relapse?" *Psychopharmacology (Berl.)* 158, no. 4, pp. 343–359.

addiction.[14] Life stressors combined with poor coping skills increase addiction risk through impulsive actions and self-medication. While it may not be possible to eliminate stress, it is possible to help people manage it more effectively.

Each of us has a signature style or styles for stress management. Our methods may have worked well in the past, and may still work in some situations, but many of our habitual responses to stress actually work against us. By learning to identify triggers to our stress and recognize our automatic responses, we can begin to take more thoughtful and more effective approaches to stress management.

Research from the National Institute on Drug Abuse indicates a strong connection between mood disorders and substance abuse. Individuals diagnosed with a mood disorder (like depression or anxiety) are twice as likely to abuse substances as those without a mood disorder.[15] It makes sense that if we're uncomfortable in our lives, and are experiencing mood disorders, we may seek to escape those emotional experiences with drugs. In fact, doctors often recommend prescription drugs as a solution to mood disorders. While prescription drugs can have positive results for some mood disorders, self-medicating is not an effective way to heal from mental and emotional issues. Learning to manage emotions and thoughts can help with recovery.[16]

Lifestyle Issues

Healthy choices in nutrition, exercise, and sleep provide the very basic foundation for all areas of health. When individuals make consistently poor choices relative to their day-to-day health maintenance, they invite disease in both the mental and physical realms.

---

[14] Sinha, R., and A.M. Jastreboff. 2013. "Stress As a Common Risk Factor for Obesity and Addiction." *Biological Psychiatry* 73, no. 9, pp. 827–835.

[15] Susan, B.Q., K.T. Brady, and S.C. Sonne. 2005. "Mood Disorders and Substance Use Disorder: A Complex Comorbidity." *Science & Practice Perspectives* 3, no. 1, pp. 13–21.

[16] Laudet, A.B., S. Magura, H.S. Vogel, and E. Knight. 2000. "Recovery Challenges Among Dually Diagnosed Individuals." *Journal of Substance Abuse Treatment* 18, no. 4, pp. 321–329.

Everything about our experience—from how sharp our minds are from day to day to our emotional health, to our physical health—is profoundly impacted by the seemingly small choices we make each day about what to eat, how much to sleep, whether or not to exercise, and how we make social connections.

The Role of Employers

The traditional role of employers, when they addressed mental and behavioral health at all, has been to provide screenings and referrals to Employee Assistance Programs or other health resources. Today, employers are more proactively addressing these issues, which takes a number of forms.

Preventative health supports in the form of tools for improving well-being, resilience, and lifestyle management are increasingly available in easily accessible digital, mobile formats. Similarly, access to coaching and counseling has become easier and less expensive. Many organizations are investing in tools for their workforce to utilize for preventative and nonacute self-care.

A related strategy utilizes data on employee mental and physical health to flag risk and route employees to resources as needed. For instance, a secure, confidential digital platform may suggest that an individual contact another resource, such as Employee Assistance Program or counseling service, for support when an assessment flags depression or anxiety risk for that individual.

More sophisticated information systems combine user data from multiple sources, such as medical claims, screenings and assessments, and demographic data to create predictive models which help employers anticipate needs in the workforce.

While some have suggested that employers and even managers need to take responsibility to address mental health concerns with employees, I feel it's critical to respect employee privacy and route them to resources without revealing their identity to managers.

There continues to be significant stigma around mental health issues and profound misunderstandings about its nature. It's perfectly possible for you take an assessment that flags you at risk for anxiety or depression because you're going through a rough patch from which you will recover

by Friday. We all have fluctuations in mood and energy which don't necessarily make us mentally ill. And, many people travel through periods
of ill mental health during periods of their lives. Getting them support
without labeling them mentally ill improves their chances of recovery.

Questions to Ask Yourself

1. Is your organization providing a broad spectrum of supports and
   resources for preventative health as well as acute conditions?
2. How is employee data used in the organization? Is privacy respected?
3. Is data collected across platforms for analysis to help leadership
   understand trends in the workforce?
4. Are there certain job categories where high-risk individuals are more
   likely to work?
5. Are there certain job types which are so stressful they make employees vulnerable to mental health issues?

Questions to Ask Leadership

1. Have you noted a rise in mental and behavioral health problems over
   the past five years here?
2. Do you think we have the right level of investment in programs to
   prevent and treat mental health issues and substance abuse?
3. Are we using our data to better understand patterns in mental health
   needs and things like their relationship to productivity and turnover?

Questions for the Workforce

We should be extremely careful about asking mental health questions of the
workforce. There are tools to assess mental and emotional health in secure,
HIPPA compliant ways, and I recommend leaning on a vendor for these.

Questions relevant to healthy lifestyle can be found in the previous
chapter on Well-Being.

CHAPTER 6

Resilience, Energy, and Burnout

Resilience is at once proactive, pragmatic, and humble. It knows it needs others. It doesn't overcome failure so much as transmute it, integrating it into the reality that evolves.

—Tippett, 252

One aspect of maintaining well-being and positivity is the ability to recognize challenges as opportunities. This outlook is one of the key factors of resilience. When a person has high levels of resilience (i.e., ability to bounce back from problems and a tendency to see challenges as opportunities for growth and learning), they have higher levels of well-being. This is both because of an overall optimistic approach to life and because they have the motivation and energy to work through issues that arise. High resilience supports all the areas of our lives that make up our overall well-being: our physical health, relationships, financial health, career, spirituality, and emotional well-being.

Resilience has become a workplace concept and even the basis for workplace trainings and tools which seek to improve productivity, engagement, employee satisfaction, and overall life satisfaction. In the previous chapter I spoke of resilience as foundational to well-being. In this chapter we'll explore it further, along with its sibling, energy.

Energy

Energy is required for every endeavor in our lives, even those we execute unconsciously. Our productivity, creativity, and attitudes at work are all profoundly affected by our levels of energy. Think about how you've performed at work when you are overly tired or sick as compared to when you are well-rested and healthy. Energy isn't the only thing that makes us productive (if we aim our energy at everything but work, it doesn't benefit our employer), but it is necessary for good work and for resilience. We can't bounce back from challenges when we don't have the energy to do so.

What does this have to do with creating a great workplace? It's important to understand both energy and resilience when we think about how to create the best environment for people at work.

Energy waxes and wanes throughout the day, month, and year. It's impacted by shared experiences like where we are in the work week, the weather, holidays, and shared workplace stresses. It's also impacted by personal variables like how well we sleep, stress at home, illness, emotional experiences, and so on.

The expectation that employees will produce a steady stream of work—that their performance will be consistently high—is unrealistic. None of us can do that, yet we often seem to expect it of others.

How to Support Energy at Work

Rhythms

Mangers should be trained to understand that there will be ebbs and flows, and to do what they can to create a supportive atmosphere to help employees weather the down times, and to support overall energy health. For example, employees should be encouraged to stay home when they're sick and to take that time completely off work for recovery (no dialing in for conference calls or checking e-mail).

Recognize (and train managers to understand) that the day also has natural rhythms and we perform best when we honor them. There are many methods of productivity that honor our cognitive rhythms, such as engaging in focused work periods of 45 minutes followed by short breaks, with long breaks several times per day. There's considerable science behind the advice to take breaks.

Spaces

Create spaces for quiet and spaces to socialize. Studies have shown that people who socialize more at work are more productive (Robison 2008;

Gensler 2008). Given that many people see socialization as wasted time, this requires a change in thinking, especially for managers.

While introverts may gravitate toward a quiet spot to take a break, and extroverts may want to chat at the coffee machine, everyone has moments where each is needed. Organizations have experimented with centralizing and decentralizing coffee stations to create intimate groups of interactions or to create more "collisions" between co-workers from different parts of the office.

Breaks and Recreation

Encourage people to actually take their lunch break and eat lunch away from their desks. It's not only better for their health, but will provide a cognitive energy recharge.

Recreational opportunities at work can provide socialization time as well as a physical boost in energy. Companies like Google have received press for indoor sports courts, ping-pong, and the like, but you don't necessarily need a lot of space to offer some recreation. Foosball tables are relatively compact and can be the source of friendly team competitions. Encouraging walks during breaks, sending out a Slack message encouraging a stretching break, or bringing in a yoga instructor once a week are all steps toward encouraging physical activity to restore mind and body.

Boundaries

Create and model boundaries between work time and nonwork time by communicating clear expectations about whether people are expected to check e-mail on nonwork hours (ideally, not). A couple of effective strategies are: (1) If employees do need to work during nonregular hours (to catch up or because they want the quiet time to think or whatever), encourage them to delay delivery of any e-mails they write during those times. E-mail can be set to arrive to recipients during their work hours, saving them from worrying about whether they should be checking e-mail at home, and from worrying about the work that is the subject of the e-mail. (2) Communicate that if you need employees during nonwork hours (including evenings, weekends, holidays, and vacations), you will call them on the phone (if that is okay with them). This frees them from checking e-mail "just in case" there's something critical.

Burnout

When we don't respect fluctuations on our energy levels, when we ove-ridentify with work, and when we simply work too hard for too long, we can become burned out. Burnout manifests as a lack of energy or interest in work, a feeling that work doesn't really matter, a sense of futility, and even feelings of resentment.

According to the World Health Organization (WHO), occupational burnout is a syndrome.

Burnout is defined in ICD-11 as follows:

Burn-out is a syndrome conceptualized as resulting from chronic workplace stress that has not been successfully managed. It is char-acterized by three dimensions:

- feelings of energy depletion or exhaustion;
- increased mental distance from one's job, or feelings of nega-tivism or cynicism related to one's job;
- reduced professional efficacy.

Burn-out refers specifically to phenomena in the occupational context and should not be applied to describe experiences in other areas of life.[1]

Maintaining energy and interest for work is a matter of learning to observe and manage the ebb and flow of our physical, cognitive, and emotional resources over the course of the day, week, month, year, and career.

Assuming that all is generally well at work (you don't hate your job or your boss, and so on, which is a different problem), it should be possible

---

[1] WHO. May 28, 2019. "Burn-out an "Occupational Phenomenon": Interna-tional Classification of Diseases." Retrieved June 1, 2019.

to manage work in a way that keeps you mostly engaged and allows for breaks to refresh when you begin to wear down.

Burnout prevention has to happen on two levels: the individual and the organizational.

Individual Level Burnout Prevention

Learning to recognize our responses to stress, emotional strain, and exhaustion provide the foundation for burnout prevention self-management. Exhaustion and burnout trigger different reactions in different people based on their go-to style of coping.

When we cultivate skill at recognizing patterns in our energy and cognition, we can not only manage the natural dips but can also anticipate them to smooth the ride.

Energy levels ebb and flow in a wavy pattern—shorter waves across a day, long waves over year, and even longer over a career. Not every day or every year looks the same, but you can establish some predictability with self-knowledge. Maybe mornings are your good times, or maybe you think best at night. You may have a pretty persistent slump in the afternoon, or tend to see your productivity take a nosedive after lunch. Similarly, you may have better and worse days of the week, and better and worse seasons of the year.

With a sense of your individual patterns, you become hyper aware of the onset of a downswing. A single thought of "I don't really care" when you've been working hard for a couple of weeks can clue you into something going on. Is that thought followed by "I hate this"? Evidence is mounting and it's time to consider a break to refuel.

This kind of self-awareness is facilitated by mindfulness practice. Mindfulness has been shown as an effective remedy to burnout.[2] It gives us the pause we need to reflect on our internal experiences.

Recent research on professional burnout acknowledges the multidimensional nature of the phenomenon and suggests that

---

[2]   Michelle, L., and A. Sammons. 2016. "Systematic Review of Mindfulness Practice for Reducing Job Burnout." *American Journal of Occupational Therapy* 70, no. 2, pp. 7002250020p1–7002250020p10. doi:10.5014/ajot.2016.016956

interventions to reduce burnout should be planned and designed in terms of the particular component of burnout that needs to be addressed. That is, it may be more effective to consider how to reduce likelihood of emotional exhaustion, or to prevent the tendency to depersonalize, or to enhance one's sense of accomplishment, rather than to use a more general stress reduction approach.[3]

Organizational Level Burnout Prevention

Forward thinking employers recognize that long hours, minimal breaks, and no flexibility are ultimately harmful to employees and the business. Unfortunately, there is no one answer to how to provide healthy conditions. Each industry and job type is different, but in the really tough spots—where frontline workers have high stress and low control—there need to be both formal policies that limit work hours and provide generous breaks, and a formal acknowledgment, or blessing, of some of the informal arrangements that employees create organically. This isn't to put the responsibility back on employees, but the messy reality of life is that what people need changes day to day and formal policies are never enough. This week I'm treading water trying to survive a heartbreak, yesterday you had a terrible stomach ache, and tomorrow our co-worker will need to leave unexpectedly to help his aging mother. We need our employers to support us to help each other informally when necessary.

An individual's ability to manage their energy is highly dependent on their job and their organization. People who can't choose to take a break when they need one are more at the mercy of the organization than those who can. In any case, organizations have to understand the value of time off, and of listening to what employees need.

Research shows that most people can concentrate on a task for 25 minutes before needing a five-minute break. This is certainly not the standard for how most people work in any type of job, but it's good to keep

---

[3] Maslach, C. 2017. "Burnout: A Multidimensional Perspective." In *Professional Burnout Recent Developments in Theory and Research*, eds. W.B. Schaufeli, C. Maslach, and T. Marek.

in mind as an ideal. The more we work with our natural cognitive abilities rather than against them, the less likely we are to burn out or make mistakes.

For individuals in low-control jobs, providing frequent break opportunities is helpful. The advantage of many low-control jobs is that they are easier to leave behind at the end of the day. If work depends upon your presence, such as working on a manufacturing line or in a call center, then time away from work is truly that.

Higher control jobs, while theoretically allowing individuals to pace their day and week to suit them, can also come with excessive pressure to produce which spills over into off-hours.

Best practice for energy management to reduce burnout risk includes taking a real lunch break, taking multiple small breaks during the day, turning off work when the work day ends, and taking vacations every year without checking in at work.

Unfortunately, many people find their vacation time squandered on no-school days for kids, doctor appointments, and the like. If employees are generally unable to take some time for rest and relaxation, organizations should revisit their paid time off policies.

Resilience

Resilience, or the ability to bounce back from problems, is inherently optimistic. It predisposes us not only to overcoming obstacles, but also toward learning and growing from the experience. Individual resilience levels are a matter of both nature and nurture. When employees first reach our workplaces, they have a baseline level of resilience that comes from their inherent qualities and life experience. However, no matter the baseline, resilience levels vary for everyone. We can temporarily "use up" our store of resilience and need recovery to fill the tank. It is also the case that the baseline itself can be changed over time. Resilience can be taught.

Resilience training provides skills which help us to better manage stress, identify flaws in thinking and attitudes, and learn to approach difficulties with confidence and optimism. Developing our sense of humor serves as a great support to resilience as well. For some of us, learning resilience is somewhat a matter of retraining ourselves from thought patterns and behaviors we learned in childhood. As good parents know, helping children manage through stress and setbacks helps them develop healthy approaches to life. Unfortunately, many of us had parents who either didn't take time to teach us those skills or didn't have that ability themselves. Some of us grew up watching role models who fell apart every time something went wrong, who blamed others, expected the worst, or dealt with stress by drinking alcohol, binge eating, or avoiding the problem. But the way we were taught as children doesn't determine our future. We can learn new patterns and replace the old.

Optimism

Positive expectations, including hope and optimism, predispose us to resilience. A study by Youssef et al. (2007) demonstrated that hope, optimism, and resilience had measurable positive impacts on outcomes including work performance, organizational commitment, and job satisfaction. Optimism is so powerful that it can measurably impact our cortisol (stress hormone) levels for the better (Lai et al. 2011).

There are many books on learned optimism because (a) it is one of the best skills you can have and (b) it really can be learned. Martin Seligman, known to some as the father of learned optimism research, identified the inverse relationship between depression and optimism, and a positive relationship between optimism and physical health. He wrote extensively on how to develop optimism, and pointed out that optimistic people are more likely to see problems as temporary, situation-specific, and solvable (Seligman 2006). The overlap with resilience is clear.

Gratitude

Gratitude, another sibling of resilience, is closely related to optimism because when we focus on the things for which we are grateful, we are, by definition, in a positive state of mind. This presupposes *true* gratitude, however. My children and I each say something we're grateful for every evening before we eat dinner. We have a rule that you can't use something that is ultimately negative or sarcastic (e.g., "I'm grateful that I only got two hours of homework and not three"). Gratitude has to come from a sincere place in order to support positive emotions and attitudes. When it does, it's quite powerful. A trick I've used on my younger son when he's in a bad mood is to ask him to say five good things about his day or his life—things he's grateful for. Usually by number three his voice changes and I see a better mood emerge.

The same phenomenon is at play at work, and speaking aloud about the things for which we're grateful can create a feeling of psychological safety. Before we offer suggestions to improve something, we do well to offer praise and gratitude. For example, "I'm so grateful to your team for creating this draft. It's really moves us closer to a final product. Thank you!" After that, suggestions for improvement will land more softly on the egos involved because you've created a psychological container that feels safe. Not only do you set your colleagues up for good interactions, by expressing gratitude you get yourself into the right headspace and will find it easier to problem solve productively and respectfully.

Humor

> Humor is an abundant and valuable, yet unfortunately underutilized, resource in organizations. When effectively wielded, humor has been proposed as a "managerial tool" that can be used to achieve positive organizational outcomes.
>
> —Wijewardena et al. 2010, p. 177

Can we count on managers to bring humor into the workplace as Wijewardena suggests? It seems a risky endeavor given how quickly humor can cross lines and cause offense. And yet, appropriate humor is one of the best balms for stress. Imagine a work team on a project where everything seems to be going wrong. Imagine the manager, or project leader, has a great sense of humor and sees the absurdity in the situation. She laughs with the team when each improbable obstacle arises and they go after solutions with smiles rather than a sense of fear and foreboding. Laughter reduces stress, and when our stress levels are lower our brains work better. Fear and fight-or-flight reactions cause the release of hormones which narrow our thinking and reduce our ability to seek solutions from a broad set of possibilities.

When I started researching resilience I created a measurement scale that included straight resilience (bounce back) items as well as measures of optimism and humor. The three constructs held tightly in a reliable scale. While I don't see humor as a consistent ingredient in other resilience measures in the academic literature, I'm committed to its importance. Laugher makes a day great, strengthens relationships, puts things into perspective, and improves our health.

The best book I've ever seen on writing humor is called *The Hidden Tools of Comedy* by Steve Kaplan. The author's premise is "Comedy is about an ordinary guy or gal struggling against insurmountable odds without many of the required skills and tools with which to win yet never giving up hope" (Kaplan 27). This speaks to the relationship between humor, optimism, and resilience. Having the optimism to hang in against the odds, without the tools, and weathering the inevitable issue that arise is funny when we let it be. I think this is why people with a sense of humor are more optimistic and resilient—they have a great attitude and laugh their way to the end—even when it doesn't go their way. Laughing at ourselves in the mind frame of an ordinary guy or gal never giving up hope also takes our egos down a few notches. Too much ego is annoying, unproductive, and creates defensiveness. If we approach ourselves and each other as ordinary people without special tools, doing our best, we're much more likable.

Failure

Our relationship with failure is central to our resilience. Laughing at ourselves is one important approach, but unlike comedic heroes, we need to learn from our failures. When we embrace failure as an important part of learning and growing, when we don't hide from failure but maximize our ability to use it for progress, we exhibit resilience. Some people prefer to use language like "prototyping ideas" or "iterating" to indicate that there will be unsuccessful tries along the path to anything new. It's a matter of preference to a degree. For me, being comfortable with the word and concept of failure is helpful. Fear of failure is real. If we can reduce that fear, we free ourselves to grow and innovate. There's a line in a Gordon Lighfoot song that says "the hero often fails." That line reverberates in my head and comforts me. The coward certainly fails less often because he or she isn't trying. Heroes try against the odds, and heroes don't give up easily. Heroes have a strength of purpose that makes them patient with setbacks.

How an organization talks about and handles failure is important. I try to talk about my failures with my work team because I realized at some point that most people see my successes and get the impression that they were easily won. On the contrary, most of my ideas fail. So, I talk about that because I want teammates to know that not only is it okay, it's the only way to get to winning ideas. I step up on the ruins of the failures for a better view of the landscape and take another shot at it.

That said, failure in the realm of research and ideas is one thing, and failure on the assembly line, in patient care, in financial investing—those are another matter altogether. There are parts of any organization where risks can be taken and parts where they cannot. Consider not only your organization and industry as a whole, but also variation within the organization.

Support from Others

Supporting resilience requires creating a community where people feel they can bring themselves fully to work. Often the issues that are tapping our resilience levels have to do with our priorities outside of work. However, when we feel that we're being proactive about our issues, our energy and resilience surge and we're able to focus on other things. This doesn't mean that our problems are solved, but it's the difference between feeling "I have a plan and am taking actions to resolve this problem," and "I don't know what to do, the problem is only going to get worse and I can't deal with it." By providing employees with permission to seek support at work, and offering resources build foundational skills and address problems, you exponentially improve their resilience and therefor their recovery speed.

An instructive research program comes out of the International Resilience Project, which teaches children to be resilient. Based on their research, key strengths children need include: feeling like they have supportive people around them; having enough self-esteem to feel lovable;

being able to offer respect to themselves and others; having confidence in their ability to communicate and problems solve; and access to help when needed. This sounds very much like the conditions of the supportive community we described earlier in this book. What works for children also works for us as adults.

Questions to Ask Yourself

1. Does your work community foster resilience by approaching problems as opportunities to learn and grow?
2. Does your work community acknowledge that energy and work capacity wax and wane across days and months and that rest and recovery need to be built-in alongside productivity and pushing forward?
3. Where in your work environment can employees go for a moment of quiet?
4. Are there opportunities for employees to socialize and recreate at work?
5. What is your organization's attitude toward failure?
6. In which parts of the organization is failure more and less acceptable?
7. Is burnout a problem in your workplace?
8. What are the policies regarding breaks and time off at your organization? Do they seem adequate to give employees opportunities to rest and renew?

Questions to Ask Leaders in Your Organization

1. Do you think leaders here are comfortable acknowledging failure as a normal part of business?
2. Where are the parts of our business where failure is okay, and where do we need to create safe experimental conditions so that failures don't cause harm?
3. Do you think the physical layout of our workspaces are conducive to socialization and connection?

4. Do you feel like we have adequate spaces for quiet and for recreation?

5. Are managers here encouraged to support employees to take breaks, turn off completely after work, and find recovery?

Questions for Surveying the Workforce

(Agree scale unless noted.) (R) is the marker for reverse coding

1. I see my mistakes as opportunities to learn.

2. I'm able to take reasonable risks in my work for the purpose of innovation.

3. I tend to see the humor in things.

4. I laugh often at work.

5. I'm able to disengage from work when my day is over.

6. I feel pressure to check e-mail or messages during nonworking hours (R).

7. I'm a generally optimistic person.

8. I bounce back from difficulties quickly.

9. I'm good at seeing positive possibilities in difficult situations.

10. Colleagues in my workplace are sociable.

11. I often feel excluded from social interactions at work (R).

12. My workplace has good spaces for socializing on breaks.

13. My workplace has recreational opportunities for breaks.

14. I often feel drained of energy while I'm at work (R).

15. My work gives me positive energy.

16. Colleagues in my workplace express genuine gratitude to each other.

17. I frequently reflect on the things I'm grateful for in life.

18. I often feel burned out by my responsibilities at work (R).

19. I see burnout as a problem in my area of the organization (R).

CHAPTER 7

Engagement

Engaged employees are more productive and happier at work, but what does it mean to be engaged and how can organizations foster employee engagement?

There are two major components to employee engagement. First is how the employee feels about his or her day-to-day job responsibilities. Do they enjoy the way they spend most of their time at work? Do they feel a sense of purpose about work? Second is how they feel about the company for whom they work. Do they trust their employer? Are they proud to work there? Would they recommend the company as a good place to work?

Managers and HR leaders are often asked to "improve engagement." It's a tall order and requires a specific understanding of what engagement actually is, and what helps people to feel engaged. Understanding, measuring, and taking steps to enhance both types of engagement will positively impact your organization.

Connecting Employees to the Job

Most organizations have lots of jobs that aren't intrinsically interesting. You can try to "connect people to purpose," which may or may not work, but even when employees are connected to the mission and purpose of the organization, processing invoices in Accounts Payable is pretty boring for most people. People in low-level jobs tend to have highly transferrable skills and be in great demand in the job market. We're at risk of losing them when the company across the street offers a new perk or just a change of pace. Here are some steps you can take to help all employees to engage in their day-to-day job responsibilities:

- Create a strong work community so that even when the tasks are dull, the company is good. We can probably all think back to a menial job we had when we were young, where although the work may have been horrible, we loved going to work because of the fun we had with co-workers. Don't be afraid that productivity will decrease if people are having too much fun—happiness increases productivity and also gives you an advantage in retaining good people and recruiting more.

- Train managers to ask questions and listen well so that they can identify when an employee is in danger of burnout or is bored. Empower managers to have honest conversations about how their direct reports are feeling and to make sure it isn't frowned upon for employees to speak up when they need more interesting work.

- Offer special project assignments, growth opportunities, and training to keep employees interested. Often even small growth opportunities go a very long way to re-engaging people.

- Recognize employee performance and create an environment where it's easy and expected for employees to recognize their peers. For many people, peer recognition means even more than supervisor recognition. If peers recognize one another in view of the supervisor, all the better.

- Engage employees in conversations about how work is done. Often people have ideas about how to improve processes, but they assume that the way things have been done in the past is the only option. When an employee does a routine task for a long time, it's not unusual for them to innovate a faster better way. Empower that kind of thinking—even tiny efficiencies can add up to huge savings for the company, make work less frustrating for employees, and give innovators a sense of accomplishment and pride.

- Work to reduce ineffective meetings (see section on meetings below).

- Encourage employees to disconnect from work, rest, recreate, and recover on their time off. This helps people to return to work with more enthusiasm.

- Finally, keep in mind that when employees disengage, it is often because they are facing challenges regarding their nonwork priorities. Employees going through a divorce, with a troubled teen, or caring for an ailing elder will likely find it hard to be engaged at work because they are tired and worried. If your organization openheartedly recognizes that everyone goes through difficult times in their personal life, and if you offer resources and support for people to work toward resolving their problems, you will not only regain employees' cognitive capacity more quickly but also earn their loyalty.

Connecting Employees to the Company

Here's a bit of good news: when employees love the organization they work for, their productivity, intent to stay, and their job satisfaction are much, much higher, even if they aren't particularly engaged with their day-to-day job responsibilities. People are realistic. When they have a "boring job," they recognize that fact and mostly don't expect someone to magically make it interesting. But when they feel supported by their employer and they feel a sense of community, they want to stay and are willing to put in strong effort toward the success of the organization.

A foundational part of employee connection to the employer is that the employer must demonstrate that they care about the holistic well-being of employees. In Chapter 4, I discussed employee well-being. Demonstrations of care and investment in people is a key driver of this kind of engagement. I have seen employee engagement scores climb significantly after the organization simply inquired sincerely about how employees were managing in work and life. So, ask how they're doing, and introduce supportive programs and policies to respond to issues your people face.

Employees care a great deal about the ethics of their employing organization. However, your company's corporate social responsibility efforts may be hidden from most employees' view. Make sure employees know about your organization's philanthropic involvement, environmental efforts, and any other work to minimize the harm business can cause and maximize good works.

Hiring and training great managers is a requirement if you want happy, engaged employees. Even the best organization will lose employees who have bad managers. Pay careful attention to how managers are evaluated—don't forget that most employees don't feel safe being honest about their manager on annual surveys or in skip-level meetings. One way of eliciting honest information is to bring in an outside party to conduct focus groups. In most organizations, employees don't trust HR to protect their anonymity, but I've found that employees are often very forthcoming when I conduct focus groups as an outside consultant. Of course I then have to be very careful about what I share back, but after conducting a large number of focus groups I can share a lot of information without implicating individuals. It's also helpful to have honest conversations to understand how managers feel about managing. Some people simply don't enjoy management but end up in the position on the typical path to advancement. If you have managers who don't enjoy that aspect of their jobs, chances are their employees suffer as well. Seek other opportunities for those employees where they can contribute in ways better suited to their preferences and skills.

Working Toward the Same Goals

Competition is often considered a good thing in the corporate world, and while it may have a place, for the most part it works against our goals. We are happier engaging in activities with colleagues than we are working against them to "win." We keep the big picture in mind better when we aren't reduced to making the case that our department deserves additional budget more than another department does, or that our initiative was more successful than someone else's. Examine the role of competition in your organization and take an honest look at how it plays into politics. See if there are ways that you can get everyone moving in the same direction. I've noticed that this feeling is one of the great things about working with startups. Before fractures and budget competition happen, young companies have a great feeling of all-for-one-and-one-for-all. See if you can find ways to capture or recapture that for your work community.

Meetings

Meetings are the bane of many employees in every industry. They have the potential to waste huge quantities of labor hours, as well as to have a negative impact on employee engagement.

One incident really struck him on this topic for me. I was working with a professional services firm and interviewed a very senior woman just before she left on maternity leave. I interviewed her again about six months later when she'd returned and she said something like

> I sit in these meetings now and I can't believe they're talking about the same exact things as before I left. There's been zero progress and I just sit there thinking "I could be doing something useful. I could be cleaning my house, or napping, or spending time with my son." I no longer have the patience to waste time like that.

Below are a number of things to consider when thinking about the role of meetings in your organization and how to make them more effective. When you do that you will reduce the potential for meetings to work against employee engagement.

Frequency

The frequency of any given meeting should, of course, depend on the reason for the meeting. A fast-tracked project may require daily check-ins with the whole team. Other projects may meet weekly. Monthly meetings are often used for larger team updates in an ongoing way. It is okay for the frequency of a meeting to change. I often see people get stuck in the rhythm of a meeting and proceed to hold them even when they aren't needed. If you can skip a week, you will save a chunk of labor hours and likely cheer a few people who would love to have that time back for another purpose. Being an effective meeting leader means remaining conscious and agile regarding how often you meet and ensuring that you only do so when there is true benefit. How often have you attended a meeting that took an hour of your time, but what was accomplished could have been done in an e-mail or two between three people rather than an hour of sitting with seven people?

Duration

There's often a default of an hour for meetings. If you can reduce that to a half hour, try. Another option is to go to 45-minute meetings, which are a bit more generous than 30, but allow for transitions to the next thing. At one of my jobs we used to say we wanted school bells to end meetings 10 minutes before the hour so that we could use the restroom and get to the next meeting. Scheduling meetings for 45 minutes also softens the snowball effect of running a bit over time.

Before and After

The time at the beginning of meetings is often used socially. While I'm a proponent of this for community-building reasons, it can really mess with meetings and exacerbate the habit of showing up late. People who are less fond of social time will often adopt a strategy of arriving 5 or 10 minutes late because the content never starts right away. This tends to degenerate and eat into meeting time significantly. I suggest shifting social time to the end if possible. That way those who want to chat and catch up can stay, and those who like to get business done and get back to their desks can leave. On any given day employees may or may not have the time or the appetite to be social, so prioritizing business up front in the agenda allows you to be sure you get the agenda accomplished, create a culture of starting on time, and still make room for niceties and relationship building.

Agenda

There are plenty of meeting effectiveness resources that discuss how to create an effective agenda. I want to suggest that we make a bit of a shift and create those great agendas earlier rather than later. By creating agendas early (possibly at the end of the prior meeting?) we can identify who is critical to the next meeting. Have you ever been on a committee where an IT person was going to be needed for the project eventually and he or she ended up sitting in meetings for six months before that time came? We can avoid that by thinking through who the critical participants are, creating agendas, and keeping good notes. Bring IT up to speed with the notes shortly before they need to enter the frame and start their contribution. Likewise, participants from meeting to meeting can vary. I suggest drafting the next meeting agenda at the end of the meeting, identifying who is critical and who is optional for the next meeting, and including all of this with the distribution of meeting notes. Optional people are always welcome to attend, or they can use the time some other way with the promise that they will read the meeting notes and stay on top of whether they need to be at the following meeting.

Participants

As mentioned above, everyone working on a project does not need to be in every meeting. By inviting everyone, but indicating who is particularly critical, we can reduce the number of attendees without being exclusive. If someone isn't identified as critical, but they feel they should be, add them to the critical list. But don't require everyone to be there every time just so they "don't miss something." Good notes can take care of that and they can be read in five minutes, earning people an hour back in their day. One of my clients once said to me "If we can give everyone one hour back per week by not being in meetings where they aren't needed, it would be huge. And I wouldn't care how they use that hour. They can eat ice cream if they want to!" Bravo to that. Give people time back so they can use it as they see best.

Follow-up

Good notes with the next meeting's agenda should be distributed within 24 hours of each meeting if at all possible. Nonparticipants should be invited to send comments or reactions or simply bring feedback to the next meeting.

Special Kinds of Meetings

You may have heard of standing meetings or walking meetings or other approaches. In many organizations there is place for these. For example, sometimes an update can be accomplished in 10 minutes or less and gathering standing keeps the energy up and the meeting short. Walking meetings can be great for two people, but it's important to take physical issues into account so as not to make someone with a bum knee uncomfortable or head out for a mile with someone wearing shoes that pinch. I've had colleagues suggest walking and ask if I'm in comfortable shoes, but that works best if it's someone you're at ease with. On the up side, I do think there's something positive about walking together—both headed in the same direction, feeling the energy of the walk. It's great for collegiality when it's physically comfortable for the parties involved.

Questions to Ask Yourself

1. What do we do to break the monotony of the most repetitive, least engaging jobs in the company?
2. How do we seek to provide interesting opportunities to people in dull jobs?
3. Do we encourage competition over cooperation?
4. Do we tend to frown on people having too much fun at work?
5. Are we creating opportunities for socialization and camaraderie?
6. When is the last time we assessed meeting effectiveness?
7. Have we taken a close look at what policies and programs would better support people at work and in life outside of work?
8. When is the last time we let employees know that we really care about their work/life balance and overall well-being?
9. Do we communicate about the good things the company is doing to help the environment/charities, and so on?
10. Do we promote people into management without assessing whether they are a good fit for managing?
11. Do we train and empower managers to look out for the best interests of employees and support their success at work and outside of work?
12. How are meetings scheduled—is there an assumed length?
13. At your organization do you tend to overinclude meeting participants so that people don't feel excluded?
14. Is it routine for meeting leaders to distribute an agenda well in advance and follow up with notes?

15. Look at a typical week of meetings on your schedule. How many hours could you get back if you only went to meetings where you play an important role?

16. Do people at your organization cancel upcoming meetings that aren't needed or do they hold the meeting out of a sense of obligation?

Questions to Ask Leaders in Your Organization

1. Are the certain categories of employees that we struggle to recruit and retain?

2. (If yes) How can we attach our most vulnerable talent to the company by providing supports and growth opportunities?

3. Do you ever worry that if (fill in the category of employees) are having too much fun they'll make mistakes or lose productivity?

4. How are employees identified as having high potential for leadership positions?

5. Are managers trained specifically to watch for boredom and burnout?

6. Are managers here trained on the programs and supports available to support employees who may be going through struggles in life outside of work?

7. Have we ever done a large-scale meeting effectiveness audit?

8. Have we done meeting effectiveness training?

9. Do you think the way we handle meetings here works well?

10. If we could get everyone out of one hour of meeting time where they aren't needed per week, we would save x labor hours (you'll need to calculate this in advance based on the size of the population) per week. Do you think it's worthwhile to take a close look at whether we could reduce meeting time given that potential return on effort?

Questions for Surveying the Workforce

There are many employee engagement measurement tools available on the market. Here are just a few sample questions to consider. Be sure to measure both aspects of engagement—connection to the job itself and feelings about the employer.

(Agree scale unless noted.) (R) is the marker for reverse coding

1. I enjoy my day-to-day job responsibilities.
2. I feel a lot of satisfaction from doing my job.
3. I see how my job contributes to the goals of my organization.
4. Time flies when I'm doing my job.
5. I am rarely bored at work.
6. I would recommend my employer as a great place to work.
7. I am committed to the success of my organization.
8. I trust the leadership at my organization.
9. People are treated fairly here.
10. I enjoy working here.
11. I intend to stay at this organization for at least three years.
12. The politics here cause bad feelings (R).
13. Competition between units or departments creates negative outcomes (R).
14. I'm aware of good things my company does for the environment, charities, or other causes.
15. This company supports employees to achieve healthy work/life balance.
16. Meetings here are effective.
17. I spend too much time in meetings where I'm not needed (R).
18. Many of the meetings I attend could be eliminated by a much shorter phone call or e-mail (R).
19. There tend to be more people than necessary in the meetings I attend (R).
20. I value the social time taken in meeting.
21. Every meeting on my calendar this week is a good use of my time.
22. (If disagree above) How many hours of meetings planned for your week are not a good use of your time? (Fill in two-digit number box)
23. I wish people here did a better job of sharing agendas and notes (R).

CHAPTER 8

Leadership

Being a leader, at the core, means being in a position of power (which is access to resources). Leaders' responsibility and opportunity is to facilitate employees' ability to be successful. Simple. Good leaders stay enough involved in the day-to-day work so that they understand the realities and can help to problem-solve, but not so involved as to hover or take away employees' autonomy. Good leaders know employees as people so they can understand when they need support in the work/life realm. They use their positions to make things happen that employees can't impact as easily because of their relative positions in the hierarchy and differential access to resources. That's it.

However, we complicate matters endlessly. Or perhaps it's more accurate to say that leaders complicate things. Leadership advice is a massive industry, probably because everyone wants to be a leader. There's an appeal to thinking we can set the path and others will follow—that they'll do things our way. But collaboration is far more fruitful than persuasion.

In reality, our workplaces are more about the doers than the leaders. The doers make the organizations run. The doers know what's going on. The doers create the culture, determine productivity, communicate the real reputation of our companies, and carry out the purpose for which our organizations exist.

I'm not saying we should do without leaders, but that we've overstated their role.

Recently I attended a leadership seminar in the typical format of leadership principles and supporting anecdotes. The principles were commonly held, and often off-target. The anecdotes are rehashed and predictable. You either have encountered or will encounter these, so I'd like to review them outside of the hype.

1. Great leaders connect everyone to purpose

On this point we are told versions of the story about the hospital custodian who, when asked about her job, said "I save lives." Another version is a story about JFK visiting NASA prior to the moon launch. According to the story, he walked up to a man mopping the floor and said "what do you do here?" and the man said "I'm helping send a man to the moon."

Who walks up to a man mopping the floor and asks him what he does? Jack wasn't stupid. And the guy is not helping send a man to the moon. He's mopping a floor. That's useful. We need that. It is different from sending a man to the moon. While some people can truly make that connection in their mind, and they are not wrong to do so, it isn't reasonable to think you, as a leader, can connect every entry-level associate to the ultimate goal of the company. If I process expense reports at Toyota, I don't feel like "I'm producing safe cars!" There are lots of people who will do a job well for the inherent satisfaction of a job well done, a paycheck, and two weeks of vacation. Not everybody needs to send a man to the moon.

The pretending inherent in these stories is insulting to people who are doing a great job simply because that job needs doing. Ascribing to this leadership principle stresses out leaders by asking them to do the impossible. We should not waste people's cognitive capacity on impossible tasks.

2. Great leaders transmit shared values

The values thing is fraught. We want leaders to demonstrate good values, but their ability to transmit them is limited. There is also the question of which values. If we want to winnow a list down to the values we all should share, we end up with an extremely basic list, something like: honesty, integrity, and caring. If we are hiring people without those basics, let's just fire them. The fact is that communicating the company values to someone isn't going to change a dishonest person into an honest one. Corporations commonly tout values such as "quality," "performance," and "people." Do these things need to be said? Will people change behavior because of them? Then there are values that can exclude. For example, "health," "fitness," and "strength." Does this mean that an employee with health challenges is failing the organization? Are they even welcome?

Furthermore, the longer our list, the more we undermine our diversity goals by trying to make everyone alike (see discussion in Chapter 3 on culture). It's likely that people from different backgrounds, religions, and life experiences will have some shared and some different values. This is part of diversity. And in any case, company leaders do not create values for people.

I think we'd be hard-pressed to find an organization today without a stated values list. Given that reality, I suggest that the best list is a list that arises out of the culture rather than being imposed on it. This gets harder as organizations get larger, but I have seen some practical purpose of company values when a company value of principle truly feels like something we have all agreed upon, as opposed to something imposed. If we all agree that it's our responsibility to speak up directly when we see something we believe is wrong, then we are less afraid to do so. This has to be an organic agreement in order to work. On the whole, the company values I see at organizations I visit are harmless, but I caution against spending too much time trying to "transmit" them. If you believe in them, live them. That's enough.

3. Great leaders recognize great performance

Gratitude and recognition are basic human behaviors we can and should model. But let's be cognizant of how we're using recognition and watch the overkill.

Unfortunately, we all sometimes forget to thank our partner for a great dinner, and we don't always say thank you at work either. My kids can learn that part of being a decent human in our household is taking their dishes to the kitchen—even without thanks. Similarly, employees know that a big part of being an employee is to do their job. If my kids stopped taking plates to the kitchen because I stopped saying thank you, I would consider that I've done a poor job parenting. If my research analyst stopped running data because I didn't thank her every time, again: problem. There are times for saying thank you, and if we identify them thoughtfully and approach them authentically, the effort will be worthwhile. Thank-you's that come from habit or obligation or that for whatever reason we don't actually feel are counterproductive.

We also need to watch the distinction between gratitude and recognition. Often it's not about "thank-you" at all. "Thank you" implies that you did something for me. When I produce research, I'm not doing it for my boss. I do it because that's what I do. If one of my employees rescues me by helping me figure out something when I'm stuck, that warrants a thank you. If she produces a great report or innovates a new process, I think it's more appropriate for me to tell her how impressed I am with her skills, her creativity, and her dedication. That kind of recognition is different, and I think more meaningful and respectful than "thank you."

4. Great leaders are humble

This one gets lots of anecdotes. In a recent seminar I attended we heard a story of an Army General who gave up his luxury housing to bunk with the troops. I don' think we need a book, seminar, or webinar on how to be human. Nobody loves elitism, and nobody loves feeling "less-than." Leaders should have basic emotional intelligence. If they don't, we haven't found (or trained) good leaders.

I recently saw a *Harvard Business Review* article on "how to be more human at work." It think being human needs to come from our insides, not from articles or seminars. Humility is about setting our egos aside, which I have suggested should happen in our very definition of what it means to be a leader. Leaders have more access to resources. They aren't better, more deserving, or anything else. We need to view leadership as a service provided to help others be successful. That's true humility and may result in us going to the end of the buffet line, or it may result in us joining a group of employees up front who have asked to discuss a problem. Being human is never a recipe, and gestures designed to make us look humble never work if we're not.

The Bottom Line on Leadership

Leadership, advancement, and "success" are all about the power structures in our organizations. If leaders spend all this time talking about purpose, values, recognition, and how to be human, they're essentially taking time to justify their positions of power as leaders rather than using their positions to support the people doing the work. Everyone loves a leader who uses their position to advocate for and support colleagues above, below, and next to them.

Leadership looks different for different people, as it should. Just as with culture, there is room for variation based on personality, backgrounds, function, and so on. Research shows that differences in leadership style appear by gender and cultural background. For example, Gerstner and Day (1994) illustrate how leadership styles vary across cultures as do perceptions of leadership behaviors. In *The Athena Doctrine,* researchers report on a large survey employees to identify desirable characteristics of leaders, as well as those that respondents perceive as more masculine or more feminine. The authors argue that, across cultures, leadership qualities associated with women constitute the majority of desirable leadership characteristics. These characteristics include things like being nurturing and empathetic, putting others first, promoting positive culture, and practicing inclusive decision making (Gerzema and D'Antonio 2013).

Questions to Ask Yourself

1. Does leadership at your organization interfere with the potential contributions of "followers"?
2. Given the leader/team structures your organization has in place, what is the best role for leaders?
3. How have you or leaders you know bought into the leadership hype and lost track of the role of leaders as facilitators?
4. What does the gender mix look like at leadership levels in your organization?
5. Do you have leaders from different cultures? If so, are they expected to act like your U.S. or western European leaders?
6. How does your organization analyze data on employees' experience with their supervisors/leaders? Are there other ways to look at these data?
7. Are the gender, racial/ethnic/cultural groups in your organization represented in leadership?

Questions to Ask Leaders in Your Organization

1. What do you see as your major responsibilities as an organizational leader?
2. How do you try to communicate (fill in something from above answer) out to the workforce?

3. What do you look for when identifying employees with high potential for leadership?
4. Do you think employees trust leadership in our organization overall?
5. Are there particular groups you'd like to see better represented in leadership here?

Questions for Surveying the Workforce

Insert the most specific reference to "company leaders" you can, according to what group you want to assess, and the language of your organization. For example "the chief officers" or "the executive team," and so on.

(Agree scale unless noted.) (R) is the marker for reverse coding

1. I trust the top leadership running this company.
2. I believe leaders in my company have the best interests of employees at heart.
3. I believe leaders in my company have the best interests of our clients/customers at heart.
4. Leaders in this company are role models for ethical behavior.
5. I'm inspired by leaders in this company.
6. I feel that leaders here are chosen based on their qualifications for leadership.
7. Women are well represented in leadership here.
8. Our leadership is reflective of the racial, ethnic, and cultural groups in the workforce.
9. Leaders in this company take advantage of their power (R).
10. Leaders here are out of touch with employees' reality (R).
11. Leaders here sincerely seek feedback from employees so that they can improve.

CHAPTER 9

Diversity

If only we could get a "do over" on corporate diversity and inclusion efforts. Research shows that most diversity and inclusion training efforts have failed. Progress toward advancing women and people of color has been extraordinarily slow, and we continue to witness discrimination against people for reasons including gender, race, ethnicity, sexuality, gender identity, religion, physical attributes, age, and a host of other attributes.

Programs that have more success helping people to accept and embrace one another are those that seek to build community. In good communities we can see that variation in characteristics as an advantage. A Spanish speaker is an advantage, as is the wisdom of elders. We learn from those with different cultural heritages, religious beliefs, and life experiences.

Somehow we have failed not only to be welcoming in the corporate world, but to even create spaces with a basic feeling of safety. People hide what they can, and suffer discrimination for the things they can't hide.

I think it's useful to consider the difference between visible and invisible identities and traits, because the ability to hide some of our characteristics means that we can manage them quite differently than those that we can't hide. I don't wish for anyone to have to hide who they are, but none-the-less, the ability to, when needed, is an advantage.

This is an area where the need for generously held questions and an open attitude toward the answers is critically important. When the goal is to understand something outside of our experience, or perhaps to reconsider a previously held view, moving into a mental space of not-knowing—of sincere question asking and listening, is the most powerful thing we can do.

Visible Traits

It is difficult or impossible to hide skin color, gender, or certain physical differences in a job interview—the first gate into a career. When a good candidate loses an opportunity because of bias about these traits, it is a serious setback both for the individual and for the organization that would have benefited from their talent. While nondiscrimination hiring statements abound, they don't translate into nondiscrimination in hiring. Studies show that small changes in a resume make large differences in whether hiring managers move that resume forward. Change the gender to female, the name to something ethnic sounding, or leave room for the suggestion that the candidate has children, and that resume is more likely to go into the "no" pile.

I have repeatedly seen diversity training programs that liken hidden traits to visible traits and I see this as a mistake. In one training, participants were ask to form small groups and tell one another something about themselves that nobody can see, but that makes them different. People shared things like "I'm an introvert" and "I have celiac disease" and "I have Irish heritage." The training went on to make the point "see, we all have something." I found it very frustrating that being an introvert was being likened to major visible characteristic for which people are eliminated from opportunities. If we tell people that they can understand discrimination because they have celiac disease or Irish heritage, we're vastly under-communicating what discrimination is. I think the point was to say "accept differences because you have them too," but it doesn't work to equate hidden traits with those that are visible, nor to equate relatively neutral statuses with those that have been culturally maligned.

Invisible Traits

None of the above is meant to imply that invisible traits are not important or impactful. The difference is that they can be hidden when necessary. Of course in an ideal world that would not be necessary.

A great community is one where people feel supported and are able to be honest about themselves. Whether we're talking about sexual preference, dietary restrictions, religious identity, and host characteristics against which there is bias, in a functional community we embrace those differences for the important perspective they bring.

Power Dynamics and Dominant Groups

It's important to recognize that groups referred to as "minority" or "underrepresented" are not just about numbers. Power is the most important dynamic at play. A white male in room full of people of color does not suddenly become the equivalent of a minority. He may be in the minority number-wise, but he carries with him the status of the historically dominating group, and this is not at all the equivalent of a black man in a room full of whites. I can't tell you how many times I've heard white people claim to understand what it is to be a minority because they have been one of few whites in a school, workplace, or meeting full of people of color. This shows a lack of understanding of the social dynamics at play when we talk about diversity and inclusion.

One of the obstacles to dealing with these dynamics in the workplace is that the dominant group is often honestly unaware of unfair behavior. If a white male experiences the organization as one that is fair, where he is given opportunities according to merit, and in which he feels he does the same for others, he may be blind to what others are experiencing. Opening dialogue, surveying the workforce, and being willing to speak up with differing opinions are critical to expanding the awareness of individuals who have not noticed a problem.

Direction for Change

More leaders from currently underrepresented groups will help not only in the optics that make employees feel welcome, but also to bring perspectives of different identities to the decision-making table.

Increasing emotional intelligence (a skill that can be trained) will also help organizations to recognize and deal honestly with deficiencies in this area. People can improve their awareness in order to notice when women or people of color don't speak up in meetings. They can develop empathy for the harder road some employees travel. Emotional intelligence supports the ability to have difficult conversations, to take ownership for mistakes, and to pave a road forward in collaboration with people who have different perspectives.

While nobody has the answer to curing racism, homophobia, sexism, and the like, it is clear that improving our ability to listen to one another, communicate honestly and well, and be patient with ourselves and each other will go a long way to bridging gaps in understanding and experience. Effort should be directed toward helping employees improve their "soft skills" so that they're better able to relax defenses, listen and communicate across differences. As these abilities improve, so will the capacity to appreciate the advantage of having a variety of voices from different backgrounds and life experiences.

Questions to Ask Yourself

1. Does our organization's demographic makeup look like the community/communities in which we operate?
2. Does our leadership look like our workforce?
3. Are there barriers to women in our industry?
4. Are there barriers to race/ethnic/cultural groups in our industry?
5. What diversity and inclusion efforts have been implemented and how successful were they?
6. Does our organization work to support the development of social skills and emotional intelligence?
7. How good are we at having difficult conversations on sensitive topics?
8. What assumptions do I have about individuals from different cultural backgrounds?
9. What assumptions do I have about individuals with abilities different from mine?
10. What assumptions do I have about individuals' abilities based on their gender, gender identity, and sexual preference?
11. Do I find myself jumping to conclusions about people based on information that may not actually be relevant to that conclusion?

Questions to Ask Your Leaders

1. What do you notice about the diversity of our workforce?
2. Do you think diversity efforts here have been successful?
3. Are there groups you'd like to see better represented in the workforce?
4. What obstacles to diversifying do we face?
5. What efforts for diversity and inclusion would you like to see?
6. Is there conflict or potential for conflict around diversity in our organization that concerns you?
7. Do you feel our employees are strong enough in "soft skills" like emotional intelligence and communication?

Questions for Surveying the Workforce

(Agree scale unless noted.) (R) is the marker for reverse coding

1. Our organization has good gender diversity.
2. Our organization has good racial and ethnic diversity.
3. I have participated in diversity training or programs here.
4. (If yes) I learned a lot from the diversity program I participated in.
5. This organization is accepting of individual differences.
6. I feel like I can be myself here.
7. There are important parts of my identity I keep hidden at work (R).
8. It is harder for racial or ethnic minorities to advance here (R).
9. It is harder for women to advance here (R).
10. It is harder for LBGTQ individuals to advance here (R).
11. It is harder for individuals with physical disabilities to advance here (R).
12. Leaders here have demonstrated sincere investment in being inclusive and diversifying the organization.
13. I am able to see the viewpoint of colleagues who are in less fortunate positions than I.
14. I find it difficult to communicate with colleagues across differences in perspective (R).

CHAPTER 10

Generations

I hear the alarm sounded over and over that "for the first time, we have five generations in the workforce!" It really isn't true.

Since we've had organizations, we've had individuals across a broad age span working in them. We could argue that prior to minimum working age and typical retirement ages, the age range was even broader than it is today.

Older workers mentor younger workers, that's how we've always transmitted knowledge and created continuity. In modern times, we've generally had people working from their late teens to their mid-60s. So what's the problem?

Perhaps we need to get more explicit about the definition of "a generation." A generation, demographically speaking, is 20 to 25 years. Do we have five demographic generations in the workforce? No. That would mean the ages of our employees span at least 100 years. It would mean that our youngest employees are in the workforce with their great-great grandparents.

Named generations (Boomers, Gen-X, Millennials, etc.) are a different thing—an entirely made-up different thing, and we have accelerated the pace at which we name them. The fact that we have given names to age cohorts in our population does not mean that we have an "issue" because there are five of them. We could call it one or seven, but the reality that we have employees from roughly age 18 to 65 has been pretty stable for some time.

What Problems Are We Trying to Solve?

Some argue that that the accelerating pace of technological advancement or different experiences of significant life events makes for very different "personalities" of these age groups. It certainly isn't new that younger people are more adept at technology than older (it has been true all along, even when that technology was the telegraph). Nor is it new that people of different ages experience different significant world events at critical points in our development. My parents lived through World War II and I haven't experienced anything like that. So-on back across the years to the beginning of history. The world changes, stuff happens, and we are shaped by different influences. Not new.

Are differences among our employees causing difficult communications? If people have lost the ability to communicate well with people who are significantly older or younger than them, then we need to work on communication skills.

Are younger employees demanding different things from the workplace? If younger generations are asking for things at work that Boomers and X didn't ask for, it's only because we were focused on other frontiers of the working experience. Like Gen Y, Boomers and X also enjoy flexible schedules, advancement opportunities, and access to leadership. As employers, it serves us better to think about the supports we can provide to everyone than it does to fuss because anyone at any age has the desire to balance their work and life or to access advancement opportunities.

So why do we clamor on about this?

Either we're skirting something or making something out of nothing. If having people of different ages and experiences in the workforce is truly a "problem," I submit that it's one we shouldn't solve. We need diversity. We need our experienced as well as our fresh young employees. We need everyone. So, let's just accept the fact that yes, we (still) have individuals ranging in age from late teens to late 60s, and then move on to give our problems their real names rather than blaming "generations."

Questions to Ask Yourself

1. What is the age profile of our workforce?
2. Will an upcoming wave of retirements bring an influx of young hires?
3. What do we do to support people in various stages of their careers?
4. Do we operate on assumptions about motivations and characteristics of employees according to the generational label they've been given?
5. Are there tensions across age groups in our organization? If so, what do people attribute them to, and do you agree?

6. Are older and younger employees effectively mentoring one another? In both directions?

Questions to Ask Your Leaders

1. Do you feel like knowledge and culture are effectively transmitted from more senior employees to younger incoming hires?
2. Do you see younger employees mentoring older employees on things like technology?
3. Are you concerned about the changing age demographics of our workforce (if there are changing demographics)?
4. Are you bothered by any differences you perceive in different age cohorts in our organization?

Questions for Surveying the Workforce

(Agree scale unless noted.) (R) is the marker for reverse coding

Note: If you want to conduct an analysis to look for "generational" differences, much of it will be based on comparing the age groups on measures represented by questions elsewhere in this book, such as engagement levels, feelings about leadership, and career aspirations. You may also compare what types of programs/benefits different age groups use or request.

1. I identify with the way my generation (X, Millennial, Z, etc.) is described in the media.
2. People in my organization communicate well across ages and career stages.
3. There is respect between older and younger employees here.
4. In this organization, older employees mentor younger employees.
5. In this organization, younger employees mentor older employees.
6. I feel that stereotypes about different generations in the workforce cause misunderstanding (R).

CHAPTER 11

Work and Family

The research and consulting organization where I spend most of my career was a division of an organization whose core business is employer-sponsored child care. I've spoken with thousands of employees about how they manage career and home, as well as to their organizational leaders about how they saw their responsibilities as an employer. The degree of variance among organizations was astounding. Industry, region, and organizational history all played a role, as did whether the CEO had children and grandchildren, and what kind of role they played in their own family life.

I met women in leadership who had stay-at-home husbands and hired help and said "I don't see what the big deal is, I did it, so can other women." I met male leaders who didn't recognize the problem until their own daughters started to juggle career and children.

There are company leaders who will invest in worksite child care because it's the right thing to do, and others who will only invest if it's cost neutral, or they can see a return on the investment.

The same variance in attitudes exists around other family issues such as elder care, special needs family members, and even the very basic acknowledgment that whatever kind of family we have by blood or by choice, it deserves an investment of time and energy.

Even as it's clear that relationship between work and family is crucial to individuals' experience of life, many organizations still turn a blind eye to employees' efforts to be successful in life outside of work. In bygone years management philosophy was "what happens outside of the office is none of our business." But that's changed, in part with the mass entry of women into the workforce and the predominance of the two-career household. If employers want to hold onto their talent and enable their success, it's important to find ways to support their success at home. At the end of the day, if pushed to choose a priority, most people will choose family over the job. When employers recognize and support that reality, they can endeavor to make work and family as symbiotic as possible.

After all, when work is fun and rewarding, we go home happy. And when home is happy and nurturing, we return to work refreshed and ready to work hard. At the same time, negative experiences in either the workplace or home environment will impact the other; stress in either domain can lead to illness; and the need of balance within the relationship is integral for improving employee outcomes within both the workplace and their homes.

Family obligations and relationships are an integral part of work–life balance, and research has shown that having poor work–family balance can negatively impact health. Employees who do not have enough leisure time away from the workplace get sick more frequently and complain of more physical ailments, regardless of the level of job demands (Winefield et al. 2014). When employees become frequently ill, it impacts their home environment; it can cause conflict between spouses, reduce positive interactions with children, and increase stress in the home. For those with stressful home environments, negative emotions and attitudes can seep into the workplace resulting in lower productivity, energy levels, absences due to illness, and psychological symptoms.

While career plays a large role in identity, studies suggest that developing healthy boundaries between work and home is important for overall well-being. For employees in white-collar positions, psychological detachment from the workplace has been demonstrated to be an integral part of overall well-being. Particularly, when there are workplace relationship conflicts occurring. The more capable employees are at leaving these coflicts at work at the end of the day, the better their overall well-being. Sonnentag and colleagues (2013) found that the most important moderating factors in the relationship between work and home were recovery time and leisure time.

Managing the demands of work and family is a particular challenge for parents, and the stakes are high. Some studies suggest that child development outcomes can be negatively impacted by poor work–family balance for parents. Wheatley and Wu (2014) found that women who were responsible for housework, child care, and employment reported lower satisfaction with life and work. Chatterji and colleagues (2013) found evidence indicating that maternal work hours are positively correlated with depressive symptoms and parenting stress for women with infants.

Parents' nonstandard working hours in particular (i.e., hours outside of 6 a.m.–6 p.m. Monday through Friday) have been found to negatively impact child development outcomes. According to Li and colleagues (2014), children raised in households whose parents worked a nonstandard schedule were more likely to develop unhealthy views of problems (either internalizing or externalizing them), have cognitive delays and higher body mass indices. These outcomes are related to parental depressive symptoms, reduced interactions between parent and child common to extremely challenging work schedules without proper support for family responsibilities.

While poor work–family balance has been demonstrated to have significant impact on both the workplace and families, there are also many ways that employers can support families, and vice versa. The relationship is reciprocal, so it is useful to view families in the context of their employers and organizations in context of the families that make up their populations.

After implementing an organizational model designed to promote a culture of support within the workplace, Fiksenbaum (2014) found that employees who felt valued at work invested more time and energy into their jobs. Increasing numbers of employers now offer programs such as flextime, shorter work weeks, telecommuting, and child care assistance. It's important that these benefits are offered within cultures of support where employees are encouraged to use the programs, so that employees don't feel stigma about needing support. Supervisors can encourage use of support programs by using the benefits for themselves and focusing on their own work–life balance, or by openly suggesting them and talking about their success as supports for employees in the organization. Organizational leadership should also highlight the positive impact of utilizing these benefits.

Employees' needs change across the life course. Younger employees tend to value work–life balance and reasonable workloads more so than older employees, possibly due to younger employees being more likely to have younger children (Mauno et al. 2013). Younger employees may value longer maternal leave or reduced work hours after childbirth. Older employees, on the other hand, appear to value job security more so than younger employees. Older employees may also be more fearful to make use of supportive programs if they hold more traditional views of separating work and home lives. It's important that employers take into consideration their employees' demographic profile and circumstances of their workforce (Chatterji et al. 2013).

Employers may also be able to support work–family balance through training programs. Carvalho and Chambel (2014) suggest that the skills and resources gained in the workplace transfer into the home environment. Examples include resilience, emotional intelligence, relationship building, time management, stress management, mindfulness, problem-solving, and conflict resolution.

Supporting leisure time and recovery time away from the workplace is also important for supporting work–family balance. In today's world of electronics, employees are typically always reachable. Encouraging employees to detach from the workplace during nonworking hours can support their efforts to recoup. Supervisors can encourage this by reducing, or eliminating, the amount of outreach to their employees during nonworking hours; and role-model this by reducing nonemergency responses to their employees during their own nonworking hours. Again, by role-modeling self-care, supervisors can help facilitate the development of a culture of support for work–family balance. Winefield and colleagues' (2014) study on 3,326 Australian workers supports this. They found, as did Sonnentag and colleagues (2013), that regardless of the level of work demands, time outside of the workplace to recover and engage in leisure activities is correlated with positive health outcomes.

However employees choose to define family or choose priorities in their personal lives, it's important to support them. In some family-supportive workplaces, I've seen employees without family responsibilities feel overworked and put upon because they didn't have family. They say things like "everyone else has to leave the meeting for child care pickup and I get left with all the follow-up because I don't have an excuse."

Every employee should have permission to prioritize some things outside of work. A baby at home is easy for all to understand, but there should also be an understanding that people without actual babies have "virtual babies." Perhaps one person's virtual baby is marathon training, another's is church volunteering, and someone else is taking classes for a personal interest. Whatever goals and responsibilities are important in people's personal lives, they should be supported and recognized by others as part of what makes that person whole and happy.

Questions to Ask Yourself

1. What supports does my organization provide for employees with children or elder care responsibilities?
2. What is our philosophy about the relationship between work and life outside of work?
3. Are leaders' ideals about work and family translated down through the organization?
4. How broad or narrow are our definitions of family? Do we welcome same-sex partners to family events?
5. How do we respect the nonfamily-related priorities that individuals have outside of work? If someone can leave work to see a child's school play, can someone without kids leave to get in a five mile run because they're training?
6. Are employees here comfortable talking about children, parents, and other personal responsibilities?
7. Do employees display pictures of family, children's artwork, or other signs of the importance of life outside of work?

Questions to Ask Your Leaders

1. How would you characterize the level of support this organization provides for people's family responsibilities?
2. If you could invest in additional supports to help people be successful in their out-of-work priorities, what would they be?
3. What do you see as the advantages of being known as an organization that supports people in family and other life outside of work?
4. Have you noticed a pattern of losing employees when they start families?

5. How do we help set up new parents for success?

6. Do you sense a high level of inclusion for nontraditional families here?

Questions for Surveying the Workforce

1. This organization provides support for working parents.

2. This organization provides support for employees caring for elders.

3. Nontraditional families are acknowledged and welcomed here.

4. Leadership here acknowledges that employees have important priorities outside of work.

5. My manager works with me to create the flexibility I need to take care of my responsibilities outside of work.

6. People here hide their family responsibilities (R).

7. Working here is not compatible with starting a family (R).

8. There are appropriate facilities here for nursing mothers (add don't know option).

9. People here share openly about their family commitments and priorities.

10. It is expected that important family issues will arise, and that employees will be given the time they need to manage them.

11. This organization has a good maternity leave policy (add don't know option).

12. This organization has a good paternity leave policy (add don't know option).

13. There are programs in place to help new parents transition out and back in to work (add don't know option).

14. This organization has support for parents who are adopting a child (add don't know option).

15. This organization has policies to support employees who are caring for adult and elder dependents (add don't know option).

CHAPTER 12

Continuous Learning

A key requirement for successful organizations, more and more, is that employees are continuously learning and growing. Unlike days past when a set of strong skills could last for a career, most jobs now require constant updating of skills, mastery of new technology, and effort to keep up with new information.

But how do we create organizations where individuals have both the will and the opportunity to keep on a strong learning trajectory? We have to prepare individuals for ongoing learning, and prepare our organizations to provide it.

Learning requires focus, mindfulness, and good problem solving. It's important to think about how we think, learn how we learn, and understand our own processes. It can be quite difficult to learn new things, so it's important to consider the conditions that give employees their best chances at success. "Growth mindset" is the term that is commonly used to indicate someone who is willing and able to learn, who believes in their ability to be successful with new skills and challenges, and who will be successful in attaining them. People operating from a growth mindset have confidence in their ability to integrate new information and try new things. They handle change well, and remain open to new ideas. They are also more likely to recover well from failures and see new opportunities for improvement.

When individuals are eager and open to learn, they are also more creative and innovative, constantly creating new connections while learning new things. Cognitive capacity increases as neurogenesis (the creation of new brain cells) and neuroplasticity (our brain's ability to create new connections) work together to improve how we think. In other words, learners become better learners the more they learn.

Research in neuroscience tells us that there are a set of basic factors underlying our ability to create new brain cells, as well as to put those neurons to use creating new connections in our brains.

Building from a Strong Foundation for Learning

Sleep, nutrition, and exercise are the foundational physical conditions related to healthy cognition. Improving these foundations is possible with training, and results in positive outcomes in all areas of our lives.

Stress management is an important competency related to both the physical conditions for learning and the more environmental ones. If individuals are not managing existing stress well, they are unlikely to be open to taking on more. They may resist learning and the change that comes with it simply because they don't have the capacity to take on more. Learning to manage stress, put issues in context, and recognize and correct maladaptive coping are prerequisites to learning.

The next set of competencies which help us to be open and able to learn includes having a sense of purpose, self-confidence, positivity, and a good support system. In other words, we need both the internal and external environments to believe in our success and be invested in positive outcomes. For example, employers expecting employees to learn new things need to respect the time commitments involved and be aware of the various demands on learners. Individuals need motivation to learn—a clear sense of the purpose of their efforts and an optimistic view of what the results of their efforts will be.

Learning does take effort. It can be facilitated by content that is consistent with how we learn best—from choices of content format (written, audio, visual, etc.) to the size of content chunks, spacing between learning sessions, and repetition. That said, as we improve our cognition through continuous learning, we learn more easily and quickly over time.

How to Support Employees to Learn and Grow Optimally?

1. For many employees, stress and lifestyle-related wellness issues are obstacles to any goals they may aspire to. Providing them with tools to identify what holds them back is the first step. It allows them to identify and focus on their areas of greatest need, and those that are foundational to subsequent goals.

2. Offering content specific to employees needs helps them to save time and maximize their efforts. Often people become lost in maze materials, just trying to find what they need. Employers can assist by providing coaching and assistance to steer them to the most appropriate learning content for their learning style and goals.

3. Be ready with more learning opportunities as their progress advances. When people improve their learning confidence and growth mindset, they quickly become able to take on more learning and challenges. Even small increments of positive change in sleep, nutrition, exercise, and stress management, and coupled with early successes in learning, open new doors to the motivation and confidence to take on more. Successes improve confidence and positivity as well as ambition purpose to continue the journey.

How do we help an entire workforce to adopt a growth mindset? We provide them with the tools and competencies to be healthy, manage stress, set and focus on new goals, and finally to understand how their minds work so that they can work with themselves rather than against themselves as they learn.

How to provide the content needed to upskill and reskill a workforce is outside the scope of this book, but this is an exciting time where organizations realize that it isn't incumbent upon them to create volumes of training materials like it was in the past. Online learning platforms, universities with virtual learning catalogues, online professional forums, and instructional videos are booming beyond anyone's capacity to catalog. While this may increase the need to help employees sort through the options, it relieves organizations from creating original content.

Questions to Ask Yourself

1. What is our orientation toward continuous learning? Have we prioritized it?
2. In this industry, how critical is continuous reskilling and upskilling?
3. What skills gaps do we see in the organization? What skills gaps do we anticipate?

4. Do employees here seem open and eager to learn or do they do so begrudgingly?

Questions to Ask Your Leadership

1. Where does the learning and training function sit in our organization?
2. How has our learning organization grown over the years? What is its charter?
3. Do you think our internal resources are successful in directing employees to the growth and learning opportunities they need?
4. Do you think managers are investing in upskilling and reskilling to the right degree?
5. What skills gaps do you see here now, and what skills gaps do you anticipate over the next five years?
6. What is our plan for keeping up with the accelerating pace of change and need for employees to engage in ongoing learning?

Questions for Surveying the Workforce

1. The skills needed for my job are changing rapidly.
2. I feel like I'm able to keep up with the changing needs of my job.
3. I am able to stay abreast of changes in technology relevant to my job.
4. My organization offers good opportunities for me to update my skills.
5. I know what I need to do to keep up with changes in my job.
6. I have access to affordable learning opportunities.
7. I have access to learning opportunities that fit my schedule.
8. I am eager for opportunities to learn new things related to my job.
9. I feel like it's often too hard to learn the new things (R).
10. I dislike learning new things (R).
11. My organization offers opportunities for me to advance.

CHAPTER 13

Collective Resilience

Resilience is at once proactive, pragmatic, and humble. It knows it needs others. It doesn't overcome failure so much as transmute it, integrating it into the reality that evolves.

—Krista Tippett 2016, p. 252

Individual resilience is our ability to bounce back from adversity, and collective resilience is the group or community analog. When we're resilient as individuals, we rely on a number of skills and personal resources to get us through difficult situations. When we have resilience as a collective, we rely on a number of individuals to get us through. Collective resilience is the safety net we weave together as a work team, a family, or a community.

Humans work together naturally for survival, it's part of our evolution. And yet in today's individualistic society, we tend to overlook the ways in which our interdependence still defines and strengthens us. We are physically, mentally, and emotionally stronger when we have one another to rely on. Research shows that people with strong social support live longer and healthier lives. And yet somehow in our organizations, we've failed to recognize and maximize this basic human feature. In fact, many aspects of our workplaces seem to actively work against our ability to collectively support one another.

One example of this is when a team works together to create a work schedule that takes everyone's needs into account. This is often cited as best practice for creating flexible schedules in settings where there's not a lot of flexibility, such as for a nursing staff.

Other examples happen every day in our workplaces, often under the radar of management, as we work together to both get the job done and help each other manage through life's difficulties.

Organizations who are moving toward a model of self-managed teams are positioning themselves to take better advantage of collective resilience.

It is related to the principles of self-organization, the belief that teams can work together in flat collaboration, and may work better when they aren't limited by the directive nature of more hierarchical leader-driven structures.

Over all my years of conducting focus groups with employees, something that always stood out was the ways in which employees bond with one another, forming family-like groups. In fact, the more adverse the circumstances, the stronger those bonds seem to be. Many times I sat and listened to a litany of complaints about the organization, management, and the job. When I asked "why do you stay?" the answer was always "because of my co-workers."

Do we have to have horrible circumstances to create these strong family-like bonds? This is a question that humanitarian Dorothy Day asked throughout her lifetime of work, after witnessing, as a child, the great coming together of people in supportive community in Oakland California in the wake of the 1906 earthquake that devastated San Francisco (Tippett 2016).

Building Collective Resilience

Below is a list of ways that we build and exercise collective resilience at work:

- When one person stays late so another can leave early.
- When you get stuck on a problem and a colleague helps you, even though it's not their job.
- When you hate a task or a project and a colleague joins your effort to help you get through.
- When one co-worker takes another to coffee just to talk.
- When someone drops a treat off at your desk.
- When someone *really* covers for a co-worker so that they can turn off completely for vacation.
- When co-workers generously share credit for success.
- When co-workers humbly share blame for failure.
- When a manager empowers their employees by focusing on their strengths and finding other ways to complete the parts of work that are not that employee's strengths.

- Mentoring one another.
- Modeling work–life balance.

You may notice that these are informal forms of support and collaboration. Much of what we need in order to be truly supported at work cannot be formalized. It's the human connections and human caring that we express. It's how we respond to minute-by-minute needs. There's no policy for what to do when your colleague is suffering a broken heart. There's no policy for when to help a colleague who's stuck on a problem, or facing a setback, or who just needs some kind words and a bathroom break.

So how can leadership encourage the behaviors that create collective resilience? In a couple of ways. First, acknowledge that it's there and that it's not subversive, it's not antimanagement, even though it may sometimes work around something formal. See employees' actions for what they are—adaptations needed to weave the web of collective resilience. Second, participate in it. There's no better way to visibly encourage collective resilience than to take part in it. Offer a bit of help when you see someone struggling. Ask for help when you're struggling. Be honest about your need for time off, for rest, and for encouragement when times are tough. Too often we see managers struggling with a lack of support because they're viewed as islands. They see their job as supporting others, but have no real support themselves. But managers can accept help and support from their teams and their own supervisors.

One of the best managers I ever saw in action was so nonprotective of her position that she would rotate it to other team members when she went out on vacation or took a day off. This had a couple of positive impacts. One, she was able to fully step away because the team wasn't without management while she was out. Two, it gave team members insight into what her days were like, what the pressures and response times were, and how the team fit into the larger picture at the management level.

Reversing this process, this manager would also fully cover for team members when they stepped out for vacation. In this way she learned more about the demands on her employees, and came to value the high level of skill they brought to executing their jobs.

In some ways, as this example illustrates, collective resilience is about understanding each other's realities. At work that can mean stepping into another's shoes. When it comes to the personal challenges we face, sometimes we understand quite naturally (a headache, lack of sleep, a heartbreak, and money worries), and other times we may not have the direct experience, but we can take time to learn about colleagues' struggles to the extent they are comfortable sharing.

Great managers have tolerance for a level of fluidity within how their teams get work done. They don't require strict division of labor, they encourage interaction and collaboration, and they celebrate when team members look out for one another.

Great managers understand that nobody operates at a high level of productivity every day. I've heard many organizations state "sustained high productivity" as a goal. While that's fine at the organizational level, it's not realistic or healthy at the individual level. In fact, it's a guaranteed path to burnout.

Not only does good management mean letting go of the expectation that everyone will perform well every day, it means letting go of the notion that every employee should be good at every task. We know that some people are naturally better at and more interested in details, for example, than others. Some people love big ambiguous problems, and others can't stand them. Some people love to follow a process or a template, and others find themselves constitutionally unable to do so. The belief that everyone should train to eliminate their weaknesses is a mistake. Foster a team that celebrates everyone's strengths, and makes their weaknesses all but disappear. The truth is that for most of us, there are some things we'll never be good at—whether by aptitude or desire—it doesn't matter. Find what we're good at, and find other people who have strengths to fill the gaps. This encourages collective resilience, because, when done well, the team works together more fully and learns that rather than being threatened by someone else's strengths, we can revel in them, and collaborate to create joint success beyond what any one person could do alone.

Collective Resilience Killers

How we run our workplaces can, and often does, hamper employees' ability to create strong and resilient collectives.

Here are some collective resilience killers:

- Expectations of sustained high performance.
- A competitive environment.
- The need for face-time, including excessive meetings.
- When employees are expected to excel at everything and aren't allowed natural weaknesses, or supported to find solutions.
- Turnover.
- Unsupported change.
- Micromanagement.
- Nonresponse to problems.
- Poor communication.

As mentioned above, expectations of sustained high performance are ultimately detrimental to employee health. Similarly, while some management philosophies hold that encouraging competition will boost performance, I believe it does more harm than good. Pitting employees against one another undermines organizational efforts. A team should have the feeling of all moving in the same direction. This is one of the advantages I often see in start-ups. When companies are young and small and have a very clear goal that is in the interest of everyone (e.g., get this enterprise sold), there is far less internal struggle. It's not to say there are no politics, or that every start-up has the kind of management that allows productive whole-company collaboration and momentum, but when everyone is moving in the same direction, it's easier to celebrate colleague's wins. A win for one is a win for all. In larger organizations, however, competition for budget, for spotlight, and for promotions can weaken the collective spirit.

Turnover and unsupported change can kill collective resilience because they may disrupt what has been carefully built. Emotions can run high in both cases. Change makes many people very uncomfortable and puts them in stress response, which weakens collaborative mindset and often triggers difficult behaviors like those triggered by fight or flight reactions.

Turnover also brings strong emotions and tears open the carefully woven fabric of a strong team. Whether the turnover is voluntary or not, those left behind may require a mourning period as well as an adjustment period relative to how work gets accomplished. Sometimes our work colleagues are our closest friends. They are the people we spend the most time with, and when we work collaboratively, often the people we know best, and who know us best. Work bonds are consistently underestimated by management. It must be acknowledged that backfilling a position is not backfilling the person—the friend—that is lost. Great managers recognize and create space for employees to mourn losses. When they don't, the unhealed wounds can fester and create disengagement, damaging the team's cohesion.

It's much easier to create formal programs than to figure out how to foster something positive that is, by nature, informal. Similarly, it's difficult to give advice on how to do this, as the "how" will vary greatly based on the kind of work happening in various parts of your organizations. Starting with the questions below should help you think about how to foster collective resilience in your organization.

Questions to Ask Yourself

1. Are employees discouraged from creating grassroots solutions to day-to-day problems?
2. Do managers feel supported to allow teams to work creatively and collaboratively?
3. Do employees hide their informal efforts to support one another, as if it's a subversive activity?
4. Does the organization treat change and turnover with true human sensitivity? How could we do better?
5. Do managers expect employees to conform to job descriptions, or do they adapt job expectations to fit the employee?

Questions to Ask Your Leaders

1. Do you think managers here feel comfortable allowing some level of informal team-created solutions to day-to-day issues that arise?
2. How can we encourage teams to create safety nets for one another?
3. How can we communicate that we don't expect sustained high performance from each individual, and that the need for rest is okay?

4. Do you think our environment encourages competition among employees?

5. How might we acknowledge and celebrate the informal support employees provide for one another?

Questions for Surveying the Workforce

1. My colleagues and I work together to support each other's needs at work.

2. My manager is flexible when teams find different ways of sharing the workload.

3. My manager is understanding about the fact that nobody can have high performance every day.

4. My manager has unrealistic expectations that I'll be good at everything (R).

5. My manager encourages my team to be collaborative.

6. My manager encourages competition among team members (R).

7. I understand the demands on my manager and teammates.

8. I consider my team to be very supportive.

9. I feel like there is a high level of trust within my team.

10. I can count on my teammates when I need help.

11. On my team, we have each other's backs.

CHAPTER 14

Conclusion

No book of advice can tell you how exactly to make your organization truly great. Greatness looks different based on size, industry, location, purpose, and personality. My goal in this book was to clarify important concepts relevant to being a great organization and arm you with the kinds of questions you can ask yourself and others to uncover how to make your organization it's unique best. Questions are your best tool for creating the path to becoming uniquely great.

Much of the voluminous literature and seminar material on topics like leadership, engagement, and generations can be dismissed or ignored. As you focus in on what's important to you personally, and as you more deeply understand what employees in your organization are experiencing, your ability to sort what's useful from what isn't will improve.

Note the themes that arose throughout this book regarding the foundational skills we all need in order to be successful in work and life. Every program, benefit, and opportunity for improvement has to rest on a foundation of basic capabilities including resilience, the ability to manage stress, emotional intelligence, self-esteem, and social support. If you try to bring change to your organization and people are stressed, insecure, lack empathy and communication skills, and don't have good relationships with their teams, the change will fail.

Ask the appropriate hard questions of yourself, your leaders, and your workforce to create an honest assessment of where your organizational strengths and weaknesses lie. You'll find that once you've truly identified the problems, answers become available. There are plenty of resources at your fingertips and you're unlikely to find any problem that someone else hasn't faced.

Ask good questions, listen well, and when in doubt, go back to basics. Ask "what is the highest good we can achieve here?" When you start there, the path will reveal itself. It will be paved with questions, and you'll be certain to enjoy the journey.

References

Carvalho, V., and M. Chambel. 2014. "Work-To-Family Enrichment and Employees' Well-Being: High Performance Work System and Job Characteristics." *Social Indicators Research* 119, no. 1, pp. 373–387.

Chatterji, P., S. Markowitz, and J. Brooks-Gunn. 2013. "Effects of Early Maternal Employment on Maternal Health and Well-Being." *Journal of Population Economics* 26, no. 1, pp. 285–301.

Dawson, A., A. Pike, and L. Bird. 2015. "Parental Division of Household Labour and Sibling Relationship Quality: Family Relationship Mediators." *Infant and Child Development* 24, no. 4, 379–393. doi:10.1002/icd.1890

Fellows, K., H. Chiu, J. Hill, and A. Hawkins. 2016. "Work-Family Conflict and Couple Relationship Quality: A Meta-Analytic Study." *Journal of Family and Economic Issues* 37, no. 6, 509–518. doi:10.1007/s10834-015-9450-7

Fiksenbaum, L. 2014. "Supportive Work-Family Environments: Implications for Work-Family Conflict and Well-Being." *The International Journal of Human Resource Management* 25, no. 5, 653–672. http://dx.doi.org.ezproxylocal. library.nova.edu/10.1080/09585192.2013.796314

Flagg, L., B. Sen, M. Kilgore, and J. Locher. 2014. "The Influence of Gender, Age, Education and Household Size On Meal Preparation and Food Shopping Responsibilities." *Public Health Nutrition* 17, no. 9, pp. 2061–2070.

Gallup. 2017. "State of the American Workplace." https://news.gallup.com/ reports/178514/state-american-workplace.aspx

Gensler. 2008. "Workplace Study." file:///Users/lucyenglish/Downloads/2008_ Gensler_Workplace_Survey_US_09_30_2009.pdf

Gerstner, C.R., and D.V. Day. 1994. "Cross Cultural Comparison of Leadership Prototypes." *Leadership Quarterly* 5, no. 2, pp. 121–134.

Gerzema, J., and M. D'Antonio. 2013. *The Athena Doctrine.* San Francisco: Jossey Bass.

Grotberg, E. 1995. *Early Childhood Development: Practice and Reflections Number 8 A guide to Promoting Resilience in Children: Strengthening the Human Spirit.* The International Resilience Project.

Jones, D., D. Molitor, and J. Reif. 2018 "What Do Workplace Wellness Programs Do? Evidence from the Illinois Workplace Wellness Study." http://nber.org/ workplacewellness/s/IL_Wellness_Study_1.pdf

Kaplan, S. 2013. *The Hidden Tools of Comedy.* Studio City, CA: Michael Wiese Productions.

Karimi, S., L. Mohammadinia, M. Mofid, M. Javadi, and R. Torabi. 2014. "The Relationship Between Sociability and Productivity." *Journal of Education and Health Promotion* 3, p. 104.

Kosawowska-Berezecka, N., L. Korzeniewska, and M. Kacrowska. 2016. "Sharing Housework Can Be Healthy: Cultural and Psychological Factors Influencing Men's Involvement in Household Maintenance." *Health Psychology Report*, 4, no. 3, pp. 189–201. https://doi.org/10.5114/hpr.2016.62232

Lai, J.C.L., P.D. Evans, S.H. Ng, A.M.L. Chong, O.T. Siu., C.L.W. Chan, S.M.Y. Ho et al. 2011. *Optimism, Positive Affectivity, and Salivary Cortisol.* https://doi.org/10.1348/135910705X26083

Li, J., S.E. Johnson., W.J. Han, S. Andrews, G. Kendall, L. Strazdins, and A. Dockery. 2014. "Parents' Nonstandard Work Schedules and Child Well-Being: A Critical Review of the Literature." *The Journal of Primary Prevention* 35, no. 1, 53–73. doi:10.1007/s10935-013-0318-z

Mautz, S. 2018. "Forbes" Accessed at: https://inc.com/scott-mautz/a-2-year-stanford-study-shows-astonishing-productivity-boost-of-working-from-home.html

PMCID: PMC4165111

PMID: 25250370

Mauno, S., M. Ruokolainen, and U. Kinnunen. 2013. "Does Aging Make Employees More Resilient to Job Stress? Age As A Moderator in the Job Stressor-Well-Being Relationship in Three Finnish Occupational Samples." *Aging & Mental Health* 17, no. 4, pp. 411–422.

Pew Research Center. 2015. "Raising kids and Running A Household: How Working Parents Share the Load." http://pewsocialtrends.org/2015/11/04/raising-kids-and-running-a-household-how-working-parents-share-the-load/

Riordan, C.M. 2013. "We All Need Friends at Work." *Harvard Business Review*. https://hbr.org/2013/07/we-all-need-friends-at-work

Robison, J. 2008. "Workplace Socializing Is Productive: An MIT Researcher Talks about the Usefulness of Water Cooler Chatter." *Business Journal.* https://news.gallup.com/businessjournal/111766/news-flash-workplace-socializing-productive.aspx

Seligman, M.E.P. 2006. *Learned Optimism: How to Change Your Mind and Your Life.* New York, NY: Vintage Books.

Sonnentag, S., D. Unger, and I. Nagel. 2013. "Workplace Conflict and Employee Well-Being: The Moderating Role of Detachment from Work During Off-Job Time." *International Journal of Conflict Management* 24, no. 2, pp. 166–183. https://doi.org/10.1108/1044406131131

Tippett, K. 2016. *Becoming Wise: An Inquiry Into the Mystery and Art of Living.* New York, NY: Penguin Books.

Wheatley, D., and Z. Wu. 2014. "Dual careers, time-use and satisfaction levels: evidence from the British Household Panel Survey." *Industrial Relations Journal* 45, no. 5, 443–464. doi:10.1111/irj.12071

Wijewardena, N., C.E.J. Härtel, and R. Samaratunge. 2010. "Chapter 10 A Laugh A Day is Sure to Keep the Blues Away: Managers' Use of Humor and the Construction and Destruction of Employees' Resilience." *Emotions and Organizational Dynamism (Research on Emotion in Organizations)* eds. W.J. Zerbe, E.J. Härtel Charmine, and M. Ashkanasy Neal , Vol 6. Emerald Group Publishing Limited, pp. 259–278

Winefield, H., C. Boyd, and A. Winefield. 2014. "Work-Family Conflict and Well-Being in University Employees." *The Journal of Psychology* 148, no. 6, pp. 683–697.

Youssef, C.M., and F. Luthans. 2007. "Positive Organizational Behavior in the Workplace: The Impact of Hope, Optimism, and Resilience." *Journal of Management* 33, no. 5. https://doi.org/10.1177/0149206307305562

About the Author

Lucy English, PhD, is a sociologist, speaker, and writer with 15 years of experience helping organizations of all sizes, across industries, to become great employers. Prior to her consulting career, she was a sociology professor. She currently works in the technology industry for a software-as-a-service company which helps individuals and organizations to build resilience.

Index

OTHER TITLES IN THE HUMAN RESOURCE MANAGEMENT AND ORGANIZATIONAL BEHAVIOR COLLECTION

- *The Generation Myth* by Michael J. Urick
- *Practicing Leadership* by Alan S. Gutterman
- *Practicing Management* by Alan S. Gutterman
- *Women Leaders* by Sapna Welsh and Caroline Kersten
- *Comparative Management Studies* by Nelson E. Brestoff
- *Cross-Cultural Leadership Studies* by Richard M. Contino

Announcing the Business Expert Press Digital Library

Concise e-books business students need for classroom and research

This book can also be purchased in an e-book collection by your library as

- a one-time purchase,
- that is owned forever,
- allows for simultaneous readers,
- has no restrictions on printing, and
- can be downloaded as PDFs from within the library community.

Our digital library collections are a great solution to beat the rising cost of textbooks. E-books can be loaded into their course management systems or onto students' e-book readers.
The **Business Expert Press** digital libraries are very affordable, with no obligation to buy in future years. For more information, please visit **www.businessexpertpress.com/librarians**. To set up a trial in the United States, please email **sales@businessexpertpress.com**.

www.ingramcontent.com/pod-product-compliance
Lightning Source LLC
Chambersburg PA
CBHW061829220326
41599CB00027B/5229